PANIC ATTACKS

Why They Were Worth Experiencing

MY STORY OF HOW AT AGE FIFTY
I EXPERIENCED PANIC ATTACKS AND HOW THEY
LED ME TO A BETTER LIFE.

PAUL IANNI

BALBOA
PRESS
A DIVISION OF HAY HOUSE

Balboa Press books may be ordered through booksellers or by contacting:

Balboa Press
A Division of Hay House
1663 Liberty Drive
Bloomington, IN 47403
www.balboapress.com.au
1-(877) 407-4847

ISBN: 978-1-4525-0731-6 (sc)
ISBN: 978-1-4525-0732-3 (e)

Printed in the United States of America

Balboa Press rev. date: 09/27/2012

Contents

About the Author

I consider myself an average fifty three year old guy. I am the youngest of four children I have a brother and two sisters. I have been married to the same beautiful woman for thirty years. I had a Christian education with the nuns and then the Marist brothers. I worked most of my life as a fitter and turner repairing machinery in heavy industry. I am not a psychologist and I don't have any medical qualifications. But I do have two very important life skills which helped me in writing this book. Firstly I have been through panic attacks and I can relate and understand what people are going through. Secondly I have been able to re-educate my brain from a young child at school who struggled in reading writing and arithmetic. To an adult who once I was shown how to use my brain at age twenty eight became use to receiving one hundred percent for many of my exams. I used the same method that I used for topping exams to retrain my brain to live a life free of panic attacks. This gives me empathy with people in my position who may think that they are trapped in a life of panic and anxiety. And those who may think that they don't have the mental skills to overcome it as I once thought. So if your panic attacks have made your life difficult or they have gripped you to the point of despair as they did with me. Then perhaps you may like advice from someone who has been through it and is now leading a life of peace and if that is the case then I think that I can help. Doctors and psychologist would have been taught more information than I will ever know and you should seek their help and perhaps my book can also help explain things from a point of view of having been there. There is a saying it is "the school of hard knocks" and I have been well educated there. I have always learnt from my mistakes as you will soon read.

Introduction

I am writing this book to help get my message out to people who are suffering from panic attacks and severe anxiety and those whose lives have been affected greatly because of it. My message is that panic attacks can be turned around into leading a new life of peace. I was once in that exact predicament of panic and anxiety, and at the time, I could see no way out. I was totally lost. Anxiety and panic gripped me so fiercely that I could barely eat enough food to sustain myself, and I was unable to venture out past the front door in fear of having anther panic attack.

If this description is similar to what you may be experiencing, then my message is that it can be turned around. From my first panic attack to getting my life back to what used to be normal took almost one year. But with the knowledge that I have gained since, I could have done it more quickly. All I needed was the correct direction and the right commitment. But then after one year, when my life was back to normal, I discovered that my normal life was not that good after all. It was still full of anxiety but without the panic attacks. I was committed to a better life without the constant anxiety that I had lived with in my first fifty years of life. And as I kept looking for answers, the answers kept coming my way.

I hadn't even heard of panic attacks until I was fifty, but looking back over my life, I had been having smaller attacks since I was a child right up into my adult life. Particularly when I was young and in scary situations, I would get very nervous and struggle not to throw up. Sometimes I would get faint. This would happen very quickly, but I always managed to avoid both. Then as an adult, on few occasions when faced with a difficult situation, I had an instant pain in the stomach as well as a very quick light head and instant nausea and I was flushed with anxiety, but within seconds I would regain my composure and continue. I never told anyone about these incidences because I just didn't want people to know in case it was seen as a sign of weakness. Then at age fifty, in the middle of the night, I had a panic attack that had me lying on the floor and thinking the end was near. That panic attack was the first of a long line that turned my life into a living nightmare.

Preface

I read a lot of books while looking for answers and methods to help me overcome the panic attacks and lead a better life with less anxiety. I was looking for a book specific to panic attacks, but I was unable to find one. Many of the books were very inspirational. Mostly the books were about how to live a better life and about happiness and living in the present moment, and about faith. I even read books about the brain. Some of these books used examples of difficult times in their lives and how they overcame these obstacles.

My problem was that, as I read about their difficult times, my mind would put me in their difficult situation and I would suffer anxiety and sometimes even a panic attack—just from reading books that were aimed at helping me. So after a successful recovery from panic attacks, I decided to write a book specific to panic attacks and about my story relating to them in the hope that my message would get out to panic sufferers.

My message is that your panic attacks can be turned around, and there is a beautiful life of peace out there for you without the panic. As I recovered from panic attacks, I kept searching for ways to reduce my anxiety, and I made some important discoveries along the way. Most of the improvement came from what I had read in books and then I discovered some important things that were particular to me, which I had worked out for myself. So now my life had become so good and peaceful and free of anxiety that I just wanted to tell people. And this book is the result. I had decided my book would be specific to panic-attack suffers.

In my book, I will give some examples and some experiences that will help explain my point and hopefully turn you into a new direction. Writing is new to me. It sounded very simple at the time. I thought I had just had the very best two years of my life so I would write a book and tell others how I did it. And then maybe they too could lead better lives.

I soon discovered writing a book was not quite as easy as it sounded. Each day I sat in front of the computer and typed away, and then after the first week I was feeling unsettled. I could tell it was mild anxiety. As I continued writing, I began sleeping less, which also detracted from my newfound peace. I decided to take a short break.

During my short break from writing, I examined why my anxiety levels rose to the point of being uncomfortable. And the answers were quite obvious to me: I was writing a book that included my past experiences, which did have a connection to the panic attacks, and a golden rule of overcoming panic attacks is to not look back to your forgettable past. At first I used examples from my youth and my school days then as I wrote them I could feel the anxiety building. So I set out ground rules of writing the book. I would not write anything that would trap me in my past and that I would have to see in print for the rest of my life, so the small examples that I have used I am now comfortable with. There would be no writing after 6 p.m. so my brain would have time to wind down before my 10 p.m. bedtime.

And these rules worked. After one week, the anxiety went. I was sleeping soundly, and peace had returned to my body. The book continued, and here it is. Hopefully it may help unravel the mystery of why your panic attacks may be happening to you so you can then address these issues, and my examples will show why changes are necessary. And then hopefully you will turn your panic attacks into a peaceful life.

Acknowledgements

I would like to give credit to the people who helped my recovery. I don't want you to think that I did all this on my own.

Firstly, there was my doctor at the time.

Secondly, there were the two trips to the psychologist.

Thirdly, all those good books I read. Here is a list of the ones I liked the most:

- Robin Sieger – *You Can Change Your Life Any Time You Want*
- Dr Russ Harris, MD – *The Happiness Trap*
- Jill Bolte Taylor, PhD – *My Stroke of Insight*
- Norman Doidge, MD – *The Brain That Changes Itself*
- Wayne Froggatt – *Choose to be Happy*
- Rhonda Byrne – *The Secret*
- Charles Linden – *Information Down Loaded from the Internet*
- Louise L. Hay – *The Power Is within You*
- Louise L. Hay – *Heal Your Body*
- Louise L. Hay – *You Can Heal Your Life*
- Eckhart Tolle – *The Power of Now*

And to my psychotherapist/hypnotherapist, Letitica Colautti.

And especially to my wife, Penny. We did it, darling.

I found the books of Louise L. Hay—including *You Can Heal Your Life*—and Eckhart Tolle—The Power of Now—to be my favourites. I read these two books many times; the other books I read at least twice. Each time, I seemed to get something new out of them each time that I read them.

There wasn't one person or one source of information that solved all my problems, but it was a combination of all of them plus my own discoveries. So my thanks go to them all. And for the first time in my life, I would also like to thank myself and my brain—giving myself credit is new to me. I realised that during all those years of calling myself names, my brain was being affected as you will soon see. Those mistakes will no longer be made.

CHAPTER 1

My Own Personal Panic Attacks and How I Dealt with Them

IM SCARED   TRUST ME

My First Panic Attack

I remember every detail of that first panic attack at age fifty—it had me thinking the end was near. I had a lot of things happening in my life and my health was down. I just wasn't feeling well. I went to bed that night with the flu, aches, and pains, but my schedule was full. There were things that needed to be done. I could not afford a rest. I woke up from my sleep as usual at 2 a.m., sweating. My heart was racing, and I was feeling sick. Now this is where I made my big mistake.

As usual when I needed results, I talked negative to myself with self-abuse things like, "Come on, Paul, pull yourself together. There is work to be done," "I knew you were no good," or "You're hopeless. I told you you would never be any good." These are the same comments that were used on me as a child, and as an adult, I was regularly using these comments to motivate myself when things needed to be done. There is no way I would speak to anyone in that way, yet I spoke to myself like that regularly.

After this bout of self-abuse, I felt even worse, so I gave myself an even bigger dose of abuse, and consequently the feeling got much worse. I felt so bad I got up out of bed, and then I collapsed to the floor. I had never felt so bad in all my life.

I made it to the bathroom to lie down on the cold bathroom tiles, as it was now wintertime and the tiled floor was very cold. I was so hot, I disrobed and lay on the tiles to try to cool down. I held out until eight thirty in the morning and made it to the doctor's surgery, but then it only got worse. In front of the doctor, I collapsed then lay on a bed and started to shake uncontrollably. My heart raced so fast it hurt my chest. I was so hot that I had to disrobe.

I had been in this condition for seven hours now. My heart was hurting so much that I thought I was having a heart attack. By now, it had built up to the point where I thought I was going to die. "That's it," I said to myself. "This is what happens just before you die." I remember saying, "God, if you're going to take me, then do it now." And then instantly the shaking stopped and I was calm as I waited for death.

After thirty seconds, I realised that I wasn't going to die, and at that exact point all the intensity came back and the panic attack continued. The doctor gave me two Valium tablets, and then half an hour later I was relaxed enough to go home.

At least having a panic attack in front of a doctor, he knew what was happening and prescribed me medjation. He also referred me to a psychologist.

My First Month with Panic Attacks

My very first three days were bedridden as I took two Valium tablets three times per day—six Valium tablets each day—just to help me cope. I only left the house escorted by my wife to visit doctors or the psychologist. I was too afraid to go anywhere in case of a panic attack in public.

After the first three days, my doctor prescribed me to only take Valium when a panic attack arrived. He also prescribed me a drug that would slowly address the imbalance in my brain. I had to take one of these tablets per day. Now at home and accompanied by my wife only, my fear was I had commitments and life had to go on. Only thinking these things was enough to give me another panic attack. So I contacted the people I had commitments with and cancelled. I told them I would be out for a month.

During that first month at home, I had about fifteen panic attacks. I was so frail and exhausted. I had trouble eating and lost six kilos in weight, and I am a slim person to start with; now my energy had been drained. But life had to go on. My wife and I had committed ourselves to a six-month project to renovate a house which we would eventually live in, with the builder lined up to do the work with us so life had to carry on.

My Second Month with Panic Attacks

Now my doctor had said to me, "If you can get by without the Valium, then you must stop taking them because the more you take, the less effect they will have on you." This was good information, which I had listened to carefully in the next two weeks. My wife was taking me out of the house for walks and trips to shopping centres. Then in the following two weeks, we had arrived at the house renovation site with the builder, and we commenced work. I explained to the builder that I was struggling with anxiety because he was a good friend of mine. On we went with our six-month project.

In that second month, with the help of my wife and the builder, I only had taken four Valium tablets—when things really overwhelmed me, even though every day I had severe anxiety and I felt very ill. Working was a help to overcome the panic attacks, and getting out of the house was a "must do," even though working every day gave me severe anxiety. But I would have had anxiety just sitting at home. So at this point, I had broken the shackles of confinement at home. I also stopped taking the drug to alter the imbalance in my brain. The doctor advised me against stopping, but the drug had increased my nightmares to the point of horror, and I stopped taking them without telling him.

My Third Month with Panic Attacks

The third month was also difficult. Every day, I had severe anxiety, as I did from that first panic attack. But unlike that first attack, now I had learnt to treat myself with understanding instead of abuse. I look back now and I think that was a big change in my panic attacks.

Let me explain it. Severe anxiety plus self-abuse equals a panic attack, and severe anxiety plus self-encouragement and self-understanding equals slightly less anxiety and possibly no panic attack. Anxiety is not comfortable, but at least your life can carry on while dealing with it.

By now, I was trying hard to deal with anxiety and take less medication. I thought incorrectly that if I didn't need medication, then I was cured, and I so desperately wanted to be cured.

My Fourth, Fifth, and Sixth Months with Panic Attacks

In the fourth and fifth months, my anxiety had lessened with only the need to take one tablet of medication after a tough time on the job got me a bit overwhelmed. Then in the sixth month, my anxiety had lessened to the point that if I didn't think about it, then it didn't occur to me the project was now working to divert my mind away from anxiety. I went a whole two weeks without being anxious or worried about something, and at that point I remember saying to myself, "I'm cured." Then within a few seconds, my mind again focused on the problem I could feel anxiety building, the heart racing, and the temperature rising. But with positive self-talk and no need for medication, I was able to talk myself back to being calm. Still, I remember being disappointed about not being cured. Six months had passed and the project was finished, and I was committed to getting my physical and mental health back to normal.

During the first two months of the panic attacks, I had many trips to the doctor and two trips to the psychologist. Then the six-month renovation project began and trips to the doctor were very few, and I could spare no more time for trips to the psychologist. I believe my doctor did a good job with me, and I am grateful for his help, and the psychology helped to point me in the right direction. The project was over now. I had time on my hands and was committed to leading a better life. My wife had purchased books for me to read, but during the renovation, I only had time to glimpse through them.

The things in life that I had taken for granted were so hard for me to get back into during the six months we had put our social life on hold. My first bus trip into the city caused me to almost have a panic attack; although I went through with it, I struggled. My wife took me to the cinema to see a comedy. I struggled with that too. I was quite anxious. It took a while to calm myself down, but the comedy helped me to loosen up eventually as it diverted my mind away from anxiety.

Our first social event together was a party that people were throwing for us to farewell us from our home to our new address. I was so nervous about having a panic attack in front my friends that it led to severe anxiety—to the verge of panic. I struggled greatly to go through with it. But as the night went on my confidence grew, and eventually I relaxed.

I resumed playing golf with my buddies after a seven-month absence. I was so nervous on that first day back, the anxiety made me ill. Golf was my pastime, which I loved playing, but that first game back was so difficult. It took me a couple of months of struggling with anxiety before I became comfortable with my golf to the point of not being nervous and being able to enjoy it.

So now I was just trying to enjoy a normal life, but it took time and effort and patience. Although I took many Valium tablets in those first three days, I tried to avoid taking them after that, and after one year, I still had many left over in the original packet. I used the drugs only to help me cope with the panic attacks, and I am grateful they were available, but it was my intention to break the need for them.

CHAPTER 2

You Can't Change Something Overnight That Took Fifty Years to Accumulate

Now I figured that it took me fifty years of negative thinking and verbal self-abuse to get to the stage where my panic attacks took hold of me and to see what damage they had done to my confidence. And it's now been three years since I have called myself any abusive names, and it's two years since I mapped out my course of commitment to a better life. And the difference between the first fifty years and the last three years is significant in my mental and physical health. So I know I am on the correct path, and I am committed to staying on it.

In the next part of the book, I would like to share with you everything that I have learnt and read about which made life better than it used to be. This will take a few chapters. After that, I would like to share with you what I learnt about myself, which made my life even better.

I Learnt about My Past

I learnt about my past, which eventually helped me deal with my panic and anxiety. All sources of information pointed in that direction; my past is where the seed of my panic attacks sprouted. My past is not to be blamed for my panic attacks, but it does help me understand and help me deal with them.

How many times have you sat down and said, "Why is this happening to me?" "Why am I always getting these headaches?" "Why is my back always aching?" If you knew why these things happened to you, then you can start to address the cause of the problem. And panic attacks are the same. They have a cause; they just don't happen. If you think panic attacks are happening to you and there is no cause, that they just happen, then you will not be able to help yourself to rise above them. So I see finding out the cause to panic attacks as a vital early step in dealing with them. Although like me you may not like what you hear at first, understanding anything is the best way to deal with it.

Now if you do suffer panic attacks and you seek professional advice like I did. It will probably begin with a trip to the doctor and then the doctor will more than likely refer you to a psychologist. I think professional help is important if you can get it. I only had two trips to a psychologist and three trips to a psychotherapist/hypnotherapist. Now they will ask you about your problem and about your life situation and then they will ask you about your youth.

Now I believe in their method many people will think talking about their youth is a waste of time. I used to think along those lines but I do not anymore. They are delving into your youth to see have far back the problem began and how deeply rooted it is in your past. Now there may be a chance that your problem began only months or just a few years ago without you knowing it. But that is why they are professional they are fishing around to work out the size and the beginning of your problem. But like me most people's problems will go back to their youth. Now that may sound hard to believe but it is more than likely where things began.

Now if you don't believe them then you will have to try other methods of overcoming your problem. In my case I did believe them and my direction to recovery was in motion and in the right direction. In my case I found out about the importance of living in the now or living in the present moment and it is essential. But also you will find out that fixing problems of the past are needed to successfully live in the present moment. So it can be complicated and some people spend a long time in psychology.

My Own Discovery

Later in the book I will talk about what I believe about my brain and how my brain works. But now I will give a small example which I discovered for myself which may help get my point across about fixing problems of the past. If you have heard about living in the now or living in the present moment it means to focus your attention in the present moment. And to try and not live in your past memories or drift off to your future life and keeping the focus of your attention in the present moment on the job at hand.

My example is if I am suffering anxiety and I bring my attention into the now and I am absolutely focused in the now I can still have anxiety. Being in the now helps but it does not always solve my problems. And the reason why which I worked out for myself in my case is; I now have control over my "present thinking brain" but my "subconscious mind" lives in my memories and can give me anxiety. Although they are both in my brain they are different identities you will just have to take my word for it now I will explain it later in the book.

CHAPTER 3

Five Things Needed to Rise above Panic Attacks

In my case, without admitting, accepting, and dealing with these next five topics, I would not have risen above panic attacks. There are people who do not suffer panic attacks to the same intensity as I did. To these people, I do still recommend looking into these next five steps closely. Perhaps they may be relevant. And to those people who suffer panic attacks to the point of despair, I urge you to implement them. Making these changes will not cost you anything. They are all internal changes in your mind. Nobody but you will know.

1. Admit that you have a problem with panic attacks and anxiety.

This was not a hard step for me to take. I was fed up with panic attacks. But before I got to that stage of panic attacks, there was a lot of fear and anxiety that preceded it. So if someone had said to me, "Paul, you are a fearful and anxious person," I would have said, "No, I'm not." But looking back, I was fearful and anxious. I was always worried about looking stupid and making a fool of myself. I always wanted to look calm and in control. I don't think that way anymore. If I'm nervous, I'll admit it.

Admitting to me that I had a problem with fear and anxiety was the first step in being honest with myself. It is difficult for a grown-up to admit this. I knew that I had a problem with panic attacks. That was easy and obvious. But admitting that I was fearful and anxious was something I would have argued against. I just wasn't brought up to be fearful. I guess it is an ego thing. Admitting you have a problem is a huge step, whether it is alcohol, drugs, or in my case, fear that led to panic attacks. An admission to yourself of a problem takes honesty, and being honest with yourself is essential as the first step in rising above panic attacks. There are lots of people walking around who say they don't have a problem with an issue so they may be comfortable with themselves, even though others have a different opinion. But I definitely saw my anxiety and fear of panic attacks as a problem, and the admission was made easy. The average person would never have picked it, although I was fearful it didn't stop me from doing things. It just made things much more difficult to deal with.

So there we have it, my first essential step to recovery. Not only was I a person who suffered panic attacks, but I also admitted to the fear and anxiety which led up to the panic attacks.

2. Be honest, take responsibility, and don't blame others.

This was not an easy step for me to take. It was much easier to make excuses for the panic attacks and blame outside factors and other people for all the things that went wrong. I could have said I had too many things to do. I was under too much pressure and other people were asking too much of me. I could have made all these excuses and blamed the panic attacks on them. Like it wasn't me. I'm not afraid other people put me under too much pressure, but it would only have been an excuse. And then after reading books and using psychology, I found out my early years had had a lot to do with the way I was and who I turned out to be as an adult. So I could have had an even bigger excuse. I could have blamed my father and those Marist brothers that bully and so on. And at first, I did. I had an even better excuse for the panic attacks. Not only did everyone put me under too much pressure, but all those people in my youth had left me hard done by, which is not the case.

Now the purpose of psychology is to help you learn about your problem, deal with it, and rise above it. Psychology is not meant to give you someone to blame. Well, that's my opinion anyway. But at first, I did blame all these other factors. But blaming others gets you nowhere, especially when it is not the case. Honesty in my recovery from panic attacks was vital; honesty begins with you. But within a couple of weeks, when I was worn out, all the indicators pointed to me. I accepted responsibility and stopped blaming others. Looking back, I'm glad I didn't blame people to their face, because I found out that once you say things to people, it stays with them for the rest of their lives.

Taking responsibility for your panic attacks is so important. You must do it to own your own power and gain control of your situation. If you say things like, "I'm powerless against these panic attacks because of (all these excuses)," then you will be powerless and all the excuses will own your power. But if you say, "I accept responsibility. I have the power to rise above panic attacks," you are well on the way to recovery.

So there we have it. I admitted I had a problem, and now I have been honest with myself and taken responsibility for my condition.

3. Make peace with the past and move on.

You may be thinking you want to get over your panic attacks and not make peace with the past, and I could see your point. But the two are linked so let me explain some of my thinking before the panic attacks.

Every day of my life, my mind went back to the past, and I think that is common with most people. But with me, it only went back to the past that I regretted. When I had idle time, my mind wondered back to my youth but rarely to the good times. Other things like watching the nightly news always triggered my mind back to my youth. On the news, I would see violence traffic accidents, schools, and many other things which linked me to the past. So while I lived my daily life, my mind was back in my youth—the darker side of my youth. I had good times in my youth, but my mind made a habit of dwelling on the darker side. I have now broken this habit.

My mind had a habit of remembering only the bad things. And that's the way my mind was before the panic attacks. I have honestly turned that around now. I have made a habit of seeing the good things people have done for me. All those other things I have come to terms with and accepted as part of growing up. So to move on, I had to accept the past and come to peace with it, and I think others do too if they deal with panic and anxiety like I did. In my case, I formed fearful habits in my youth to deal with fear when I was young, and as I grew older, I did not break all of these youthful habits. I did not break the fearful memories of these times, as I would continually look back on them with resentment and anger. And that is why it was necessary to make peace with the past and to move on to break the connection to my youth.

Later, in the section called "Rewriting the Past," I will explain the method that I used and moved on.

So now I have admitted I had a problem and I have taken responsibility, and I have made peace with my past.

4. Forget about the future and learn to accept whatever comes your way.

It is much easier to see the connection between panic attacks and the future—after all, we all want a good future. Before the panic attacks, if my mind was not dwelling on my regrettable past, then my mind was stuck on my future. I will spend more time later on how I overcame my problem of my mind being stuck in the future.

When my mind dealt with the future, my mind used my old fearful habits and memories of my youth to deal with it. That was the connection of my anxiety. When I was thinking of the future, the anxiety of the past would be foremost in my mind. But having my mind stuck in the future was a huge contributor to my panic attacks. I had to learn to accept the future for whatever it was going to be. The night I had my first big panic attack, my biggest concern was how I was going to deal with all these things in my immediate future.

I had a bad habit at looking at all the worst things that might happen and then dealing with them mentally to solve problems before they even arose. But I had so much happening that when I added up all the worst things that could happen, they added up to a panic attack. And the future was not even here yet.

So now I practically never delve into my future. My attitude now is this: when the future arrives, I will deal with it then. Of course, I deal with the future sensibly. For example, if I have an appointment at 10 a.m., I will leave enough time to get there, take whatever I need to get through the day, but that is all that I do. I don't rehearse all the bad things that can happen and live them out emotionally before I get there.

So now I have admitted I have a problem. I have taken responsibility. I have made peace with the past, and I have accepted my future.

5. Have faith and learn to trust life.

The first four steps were very important to me, but unless I added faith and belief that these other steps combined with my new trust in life were going to work, then my success to rise above panic attacks would have been limited. There are many types of faith, and faith in rising above panic attacks is everything. There is faith in God, faith in oneself, faith in life, or faith in the universe. To me, all these faiths are equal. After reading Louise L. Hay's *You Can Heal Your Life,* it was my faith in the universe along with the other four steps which got my life back to normal.

I was and I am committed to the path that I am on, these five steps got my life back to normal in less than one year. Then a few months later my life was slightly better than it had been. But it still had room for improvement although the panic attacks had stopped I still had fear and anxiety. And I was committed to further improvement; the positive results which had come to me opened my eyes to an even better life. And these results were my reward for having faith in my ability and my reward was a better life, and what could be more rewarding than that a better life?

The five steps were essential for me to rise above panic attacks and they did work for me and I believe if others committed to these five essential steps they too will rise above panic attacks and life begins to be normal again. Perhaps you are thinking to yourself I had a good youth I don't need to make changes I don't have any problems just panic attacks I just want to get rid of panic attacks. Then that's OK just read on we are all different perhaps you will see similarities along the way. And perhaps you will see many aspects of the book helpful to you maybe some of my examples will point you in a direction. But try to keep an open mind until you have finished the book and got the whole picture.

As I discovered my normal life was full of anxiety so I would like to incorporate many other topics for a better life which helped me rise up to a life of peace and joy. So now I have completed the five essential steps before I believe real progress could be made in my quest to rise above panic attacks. A very important step for me was to understand about education and about my education and my beliefs which led to my way of thinking. As I began to understand these important pieces of information the pieces to my jigsaw puzzle of life began to come together.

Chapter 4

Thinking

Education

I need to explain the importance of education and the connection to panic attacks. If you had a fearful education not only at school but at home like I did, there could be a small connection to your panic attacks like there was with my panic attacks. And if there is, it will need to be explained so you can correct the mistakes of the past. So I will tell you the story of my education, and perhaps you may see a useful connection in your education. If you think that I am telling you too much information about education, then bare with me things will be explained it is part of a bigger picture.

I had a traditional Christian education at Catholic schools in the 1960s and the 1970s. My first five years were at a convent school being taught by the nuns. I liked convent school; I was a slow learner, and as a child, I had a problem paying attention. I was in a few remedial classes trying to catch up at convent school usually with just a few other kids.

From grade five to grade ten I went to the Marist Brothers Schools. I started at age nine and completed my school-leaving certificate at age fifteen. I was one year younger than most other students in the class. I remember my very first day at Marist Brothers; we were taught how to dress correctly how to address the Brothers how to assemble and how to march. They even had a drum band to march to all this, and we hadn't even started our first class I remember being impressed it reminded me of those movies on TV with soldiers and armies and precision marching. And I can remember my very last day six years later I was so glad to leave as I walked down the road and I said to myself, "No matter how tough life gets I will always remember how much I hated school."

Hate is something I have had to get out of my vocabulary. There is no room for hate in the life that I have now. In my very first week at the Marist Brothers school my old problem arose. I was caught not paying attention. I found out very early on that day the penalty for not paying attention was four cuts of the cane, and as a nine-year–old, the cane was something new to me. Exactly one year later, my first week in the sixth grade, my old problem again I was caught out not paying attention. Another four cuts of the cane but this time a much uglier scene of screaming and verbal abuse to accompany the cane. A punishment that I received regularly over the next six years to be fair to the Brothers I respected half of them they were good guys who didn't derive any pleasure from punishing students but that didn't stop them caning you rules were rules and no one who broke the rules escaped the cane. Of the other half I was afraid of them some of the brothers had fits of rage when they caned you and it was very scary indeed and I couldn't respect someone I also feared. And then there was a couple of brothers who scared me so much that I had trouble with my stomach trying to not throw up. When they stood over you and looked down and began screaming at you I would start to tremble. And I considered myself to be one of the tougher kids at school but these brothers almost gave me an ulcer. There were many times when we were caned only on the suspicion of have done something wrong. Like someone speaking in the classroom while the teacher had his back turned and numerous other minor examples. Many times in my six years I was caned because I could not tell on a fellow student and the punishment was always four cuts of the cane. And I must say in the six years I was there no other kid told on any other student which makes me proud of them Aussie kids don't tell. This seemed to add to some brother's anger and rage as they caned large numbers of students to find the one culprit. Looking back now I see that caning large numbers of students helped some brothers deal with their anger and emotional issues. Then there were times when the teacher was already furious before a class began and it seemed he was looking for an excuse to vent his anger. When this was the case I would be afraid from the beginning of the class and when I was that afraid fear prevented me from paying attention.

We also had a small number of teachers in high school who were non Marist Brothers I respected all of them they were good guys. When we had a class from one of these teachers it was like a forty minute holiday from the brothers. My woodwork teacher was also a non Marist Brother I had so much respect for him one year after leaving school I went back to see him and tell him how successful I was at work. He also gave me some good advice when I was fifteen, I was becoming a bit wild and beginning to rebel against over punishment from the brothers he took me aside spoke respectfully to me and advised me to take it easy. Coming from him I listened and took this good advice, if it had come from a screaming Marist brother I may have rebelled against it as I was gaining in confidence against punishment as I grew older. And I'm sure my old woodwork teacher would be proud of me now because woodwork is my hobby I have made almost all the furniture in our house.

These day's young students with attention problems are dealt with much differently than I was. I can testify that fear based education doesn't cure attention problems it only adds to them. I am sure many people have seen a movie where an adult screams at a child and then tells the child to repeat what was said and the child is unable to remember even though it was said ten seconds earlier. Well that child was me and when you're young mind is occupied with fear you only hear yelling and screaming but not the information that they are trying to convey. I had friends in other non Marist schools with similar grades to mine who had never received the cane I was so envious of them. Later in life, I learnt that the words and the rage that usually accompanied the cane have the greatest effect on you and I now agree.

So I would like to move into some very interesting subjects which explain everything about my education I am really looking forward to sharing this with you. Until the age of twenty-eight I had an opinion of myself as being not very intelligent. As lots of kids at school when a teacher or a parent calls you an idiot or stupid or dumb if you hear it long enough then you may start to believe it. In my case I did believe it in my last year of school we were sent to vocational guidance it was to help us find a career in life which was meant to help us find a job which suited our academic qualifications. I was told because I was good at woodwork to look for a job as a cabinetmaker or a carpenter. I was also told that fitter and turner was too hard for me and electrician was out of my league. So when I looked for jobs after leaving school I was unable to find work as a carpenter or cabinetmaker but I did accept a job as a fitter and turner. During my fitter and turner apprenticeship I received some good marks and only failed one subject which contained maths and algebra I repeated it the following year to complete my apprenticeship. But I worked very hard and I studied hard because I remembered being told that fitter and turner was too hard for me.

` At age twenty-eight I was given an opportunity to do a course called New Age Thinking and this course turned my life around I went from thinking I was stupid to knowing I am a highly intelligent person who could pass anything that I put my mind to. I have much to tell you about New Age thinking so it appears as an item of its own later in the book.

Education and Love versus Fear

Well, I've just told you about where I was educated now I would like to tell you what I have learnt about education. If you are thinking that you would just like to find out how to get rid of panic attacks then be patient. Because getting rid of panic attacks I found is about re-educating yourself and it is never too late to start I believe fear was a big factor in my education,

There is a saying in life it is "Taught the fear of God." I see many quotes in the Old Testament of the Bible where men were described as "good men" because they feared God. Well, if that was the case then I was a "good boy" because I feared God more than I feared my father, and more than I feared the Marist Brothers. Although obviously I have never met God I had learnt all about hell and what would happen to me if I did not obey the rules.

I have learnt over the years that to be good at anything it helps if you like what you are doing and that is common knowledge. And to be really good at something you have to really enjoy or even love what you ARE doing. That is why we are learning about education I had to re-educate myself to learn how to love life. I have learnt that when it comes to education if your mind is preoccupied with fear, then the information which you are being given just does not go to where it should and that is your brain. Your brain does what it was designed for, your brain wants to protect you consequently the information that you are meant to be learning doesn't go into your brain, because your brain is preoccupied with your fear and is busy putting you into survival mode. This is only my theory on fear-based education but I know from my experience that is exactly what was happening to me.

There was a lot of fear-based education not only at my school but at other schools also. The cane and other forms of corporal punishment where band in schools about ten years after I had completed my high school education. So there are a lot of people out there were fear played a part in their education and they may not have achieved their potential and it may have also left a mark on their subconscious that they are unaware of. That is why I am giving examples of my education to see if you may have some similarities.

An example of my fear education the teacher is at the front of the classroom and pacing the floor wielding his cane to stamp his authority and command your respect he likes to raise his voice to assert his authority. A common habit is to wield the cane into the blackboard or into the robes that he is wearing to make intimidating sounds to acquire your attention. Even though you are at school and you should be learning fear is grabbing your attention. But you cannot take your attention away from the fear and noise that the teacher is instilling. And the information he is trying to teach you is not even being heard or registered in your fearful ten-year-old mind. You fearful mind is concentrating on the fear that the teacher is generating. Next the teacher points the cane at you and in his loud intimidating voice says "You where are we up to" and you are unable to respond even though you were watching the teacher. And once again you are caught not paying attention during the entire class you have felt ill with a sick feeling in your stomach and now you are about to receive four cuts of the cane. Because you have been caught out before by this teacher he loses his control when punishing you and those insults and punishment and humiliation you received have stuck with you your entire life. And the reason that you are unable to learn is because you are so afraid that your brain has other higher priorities of survival over education. The teacher misinterprets your inability to learn while you are fearful as not paying attention and he takes it personally which is reflected in his verbal insults then he decides to make an example of you in front of the other forty students in the class. I am speaking from firsthand experience that kid was me.

Let's look at education without fear. You are sitting in a classroom and you are comfortable and relaxed. Now your education is totally up to you and your teacher. Firstly, it's up to how interested you are and how much you want to learn. Secondly, it's up to how good and how skilfully the teacher can get his message across. So there are two elements that need to work: a good skilful teacher and an interested student. And if the teacher works out how to make education fun and enjoyable then you are off to a great start.

Now let's look at education; if you love learning you will learn. There will be no fear and you will be hanging onto ever word the teacher says. As you learn you begin growing in confidence and the results you get become your incentive to keep learning and your love of learning grows. This was my experience in learning once that I was taught how to use my brain correctly to learn at age twenty-eight. The problem is how many people love learning we learn because it is the system. You start at school maybe you go further or then get a job in which case you have to learn about the job. After school I didn't like learning because I was afraid to fail and look stupid, but I was a good worker and was sent on some courses to learn new skills.

New Age Thinking

When I was twenty-eight years old the company that I was working for could see that I had potential. So they sent me on a four-day course called "New Age thinking." These days there is a lot of New Age thinking information in books it covers a wide range of topics the New Age seminar that I attended was based on the use of the brain and how the correct use of the brain can help you. Now that was twenty-five years ago and it was the first time in my entire life that education was truly fun. You see when I was at school I was labelled a slow learner in my very early years I was always in remedial reading classes and I do admit my spelling and math were terrible at that time. If you start off slow and not picking up the first vital step in a subject then everything they try to teach you after that, are just adding to your confusion.

My point in showing you about my new education after New Age thinking is to get you enthusiastic about re-educating your thinking to turn your brain into the correct intelligent positive brain that it was intended to be.

New age thinking taught us things like; thinking outside the square—there is more than one way to solve a problem—looking at things differently—seeing someone else's point of view—helping you to reach your own potential—bring the best out of an employee—peoples different personalities and how to deal with them—affirmations—setting goals—positive thinking—how the brain processes information—how to retain memory—how to study to pass exams—the importance of making learning a fun experience. It was about opening yourself to new possibilities and how to be a better person. But my favourite subjects were how the brain processes information and how to retain memory and how to study for exams and how the brain works.

I was working for a major airline company in Sydney 1988 when these people attend the work place for a four day seminar. I don't know if these people are still around but if you are out there and read this book I want you to know that you changed my life for the better. I went from a student at school who could not pay attention and labelled slow and stupid, to an adult who became used to receiving 100 percent for his exams. After New Age thinking, I went back to technical college for about another four years and topped almost every exam I sat. I am not boasting but I discovered I could pass anything I put my mind to. These are some of the same brain skills I would like you to adopt to turn your brain around into loving your life.

For example, as a teenager I did an apprenticeship in Fitting and Machining. Three years at technical college with an average pass of 70 percent and failed maths in the second year and had to pass it the following year. Then as an adult aged thirty-three I committed to another three-year electrical trade course. At vocational guidance in my last year at school I was told that the electrical trade was out of my league so do not even consider it. Over the three years at tech I managed 100 percent for ten subjects and average over 95 percent for the twenty-four subjects that made up the entire three-year course.

Thank you to the people who taught me New Age thinking you proved that I wasn't stupid. I wish that New Age thinking and how to use your brain was taught to young children at school. Every person is highly intelligent it took New Age thinking to prove it to me.

This teacher was a highly trained person and his skill was getting his message across without the need for violence and insults. Right at the start of the New Age thinking course, the teacher said, "There is no pass or fail in this course." Immediately I was relieved, even comfortable. Then he told us the subjects of the next four days, and when he got to the bit where he said, "We will teach firstly how you're brain works, then how to retain information and how to study to pass exams," I was so excited. I couldn't wait, then I thought, "But I'm not intelligent. What if I don't get it?" So I expressed my concerns to the teacher, and he just smiled and said, "There are no dumb people. Everyone is intelligent. You will soon find out."

Just like you are about to find out, there is no pass or fail when recovering from panic attacks, and you are intelligent and you will rise above them.

I loved that course, and I absorbed all the information I could. I was so happy. I told everyone how good it was. During my school years, I could not understand algebra; A times B equals C meant nothing to me. The math in the three-year electrical trade revolved around algebra and trigonometry, my two old weak spots. Now not only could I do these subjects, I usually got 100 percent for them. When I was struggling with panic attacks, just like algebra I did not know where to begin. I was lost. Then I worked them out after being pointed in the right direction. And now my life has turned around to peace and a love for life. That is why education is so important. If you are like I was when I walked around thinking I was poorly educated calling myself stupid or useless every time I made a mistake, and punishing myself with verbal insults that damaged my own subconscious mind, then you have to be re-educated to believing that you are an intelligent human being.

It was a combination of my knowledge that I learnt from New Age thinking and the new knowledge that I gained from reading books on the brain and positive lifestyle books that I pieced together, which turned my thinking around to overcome panic attacks and lead a much better life without the overwhelming anxiety.

I have given some examples of New Age thinking in the chapter of the brain because they are so closely linked. If you are getting interested, you will love the next subject: the brain.

The Brain

Though negative thinking was an important aspect during my panic attacks, two of the books I read in my recovery were about the brain. They were the *The Brain That Changes Itself* by Norman Doidge, MD, and *My Stroke of Insight* by Jill Bolte Taylor, PhD. I have two important quotes, one from each book, which played an important role in my new outlook.

This along with my knowledge of how the brain works and how the brain retains information from my New Age thinking days, I was able to set myself on the road to recovery. Now I am not medically educated, so I will not pretend to be an expert and use any complicated medical language. I will keep this as simple as possible. What I know technically about the brain can be summed up in one paragraph using simple terms. After I describe what I know about the brain, I will explain briefly what I was taught in New Age thinking of how the brain works and how to use your brain. These two pieces of information can be used to train your brain in learning how to love life. Because once you love life, panic attacks will be a bridge you crossed to a new appreciation of life.

The easiest description I can give of the brain goes like this. There are two sides to the brain: the right hemisphere and the left hemisphere. But we will just call it the brain; the brain processes information in different parts. Between these different parts of the brain, we have pathways in which the information travels. These pathways are called networks. Now that is all we need to know. It is the pathways and networks that we are interested in to rebuild our positive network in our brain.

I think we have all heard the saying "a well-worn path." This is hugely important when it comes to the brain. Your negative network has become a well-worn path.

I could not describe this technically because I am out of my depth, but I will try by using a description. Let's say negative thoughts travel down negative pathways. We all know what happens to well-worn pathways— they become wider and easier to travel, and then an increase in traffic will soon follow. It is the same with negative information in your brain. The negative paths become easier to travel, and soon the increase in negative information will follow. On the land, paths between cities become roads then highways then dual roads and even shortcuts then superhighways. Your brain is the same. Your negative thoughts travel down the negative pathways. And if all your thoughts are always negative, soon you will have a negative superhighway in your brain, complete with shortcuts to handle the heavy loads of negative traffic. And these shortcuts will be through your redundant positive network. So the more you use your negative highway in your head, the bigger the negative network becomes. I found that the negative network in my brain had become a negative superhighway with an insatiable appetite to grow, and it was devouring what had been left over of my positive brain network.

Now we all know what happens to pathways which are not used. They become overgrown then redundant then they cease to exist, and this is exactly what happens to the positive network in your brain if you do not use it. Your positive network will cease to exist and your defence against panic attacks needs a positive network in your brain. There would have been a time when your positive network was at least equal or greater than your negative network. Then the imbalance in your brain becomes too great for your positive network and it is overpowered by the negative network. Over time, the negative pathways in your brain become greater in number. They become larger. Now they are so great they have developed shortcuts between parts of the brain to transport the negative information quicker. These shortcuts go right through your old redundant positive network and the damage is now being multiplied. These negative thoughts are so great now that they are taking up space where the positive thoughts used to live. That's my explanation of something more complicated I compared it to highways to help you draw a picture in your mind that you can relate to.

That is why when you first begin trying to turn your thinking around to being positive. It is so difficult to begin with, because of the huge imbalance in size between your positive and your negative networks. Your now more powerful negative network will reject any positive thoughts. If you tell a very negative person to start thinking positive, he or she will usually snap back with some form of negative comment and perhaps even aggression. That's how powerful the negative network has become; it has overpowered his or her thinking, and his or her automatic response is negative.

When these negative thoughts start taking over, parts of our body are overwhelmed by them, which can become emotions like feeling anger or anxiety or even involuntary body movements. Like our heart will beat faster and we will begin to perspire or our breath will become shorter and faster or we will twitch or tremble. All these symptoms, and all we did was thinking too many negative thoughts. The next thing you know, you are suffering anxiety or rage. And if you persist with the negativity and let you negative superhighway take over, it will develop into a panic attack.

But wait there is good news if you are willing to change your negative thinking ways. The technical term is called "brain plasticity," which means you moulded your brain over time into a negative thinking machine. Now it can be un—moulded and remoulded into a positive thinking machine, and it can be turned around quite quickly. But that turning point is up against your now dominant negative superhighway and it may be harder than it sounds at first. So you must be patient and persistent with your positive thinking. It still needs to be done correctly, and we will cover that later in the book. When I discovered brain plasticity, I set about opening up all those positive brain pathways that had been overgrown and overtaken by the negative ones and it worked and is continually working.

That was my explanation of the positive and negative networks in your brain. Now if you read books on the brain, you will find very big words and other explanations, and I may differ to them. But I described it as I did, because I was taught if you want to remember something, then associate an image with a name. And I want you to picture the positive network in your brain building in size and once again dominating the negative network.

Now at this point I would like to quote two people whose information I swear by. I have used these two pieces of information from the moment I read them. Firstly, from Jill Bolte Taylor, PhD. She says in her book *My Stroke of Insight,* "Once an emotional circuit is triggered like anger it takes ninety seconds for the chemical produced by the brain to run through the body and flush out of the system completely."

I have definitely found this to be true in my experience of fear. When I have had that instant flush of anxiety after anger or a fearful thought, I now know to be patient and that relief will come soon if I get into my positive network. Secondly, I would like to write some information from Norman Doidge, MD, in his book *The Brain That Changes Itself.* He is quoting a UCLA psychiatrist, Jeffrey M. Schwartz. This is not an exact quote but a summary of a few sentences in my own simple language. "Building up the positive circuitry will eventually make the old negative circuitry redundant." He also recommends adding a positive feeling or emotion with the positive circuitry. I like to smile when I do this. It goes on to say, "It should also be done regularly so eventually it becomes automatic." I hope my summary of these quotes has done these three people justice because I believe in them 100 percent and my thanks goes to them.

Now remember during the New Age thinking seminar that I was taught how my brain works to process memory and how the brain retains information. And that information turned me around from a stupid little boy with not much hope to a highly intelligent adult who loved getting 100 percent for his exams. I was taught how the brain processes information, how to study for exams, and how to retain memory. Now I used these skills along with these two beautiful pieces of information from the books of Jill Bolte Taylor, PhD, and Norman Doidge, MD, to turn my brain into a positive thinking machine and to block negativity. So when a negative emotion of fear arrived, like that instant punch in the stomach that many of us have felt, I constantly delved into my new positive circuitry and remained patient for ninety seconds or until the immediate danger of being overcome had disappeared. Sometimes it only took a couple of seconds to regain control. Then it was up to me to continually, positively self-talk until all was well again.

It worked back then in my recovery days, and I rarely have had to use it since. These days when negative emotions arise, it works each time, but only because I truly believe in it and I TRUST it. You can be saying positive words to yourself, but you have to believe in them and add that smile to them as you say them. If you are just reading words parrot fashion in the hope that they might work, then you are only heading in the right direction but not getting the good results that you could be.

I am constantly working on my positive superhighway, all day, every day, simply by smiling my way through the day and thinking of loving life and loving my life. New Age thinking taught me some very important skills of how the brain processes information, and these skills have served me well. Here are a few examples.

How the Brain Processes Information

I was taught the brain processes information on a last-in, first-out basis. That means the last thing you heard will be the first thing you remember.

That's if you were paying attention and not fearful. An example is you see someone walking down the street and you say to yourself, "Hey I know that guy. What is his name?" but you can't remember and then you forget about it. Sometime later, maybe hours or even days, you remember that his name is Ralph even though you were completely focused on something else. The answer just appeared in your head and you had totally forgotten about it. The reason you eventually remembered his name is because you asked your brain a question. Your brain does not forget that you asked a question, only you forgot that you asked. That is how you extract knowledge from your brain, simply asking your brain a question. The reason it took so long was the information was stored behind ten years of information. But your brain knew the answer; a well-trained brain will always give you what you want.

Secondly, there are sayings like "Picture this" or "Getting a picture in my mind." These sayings are no coincidence. If you want to remember something, associate a picture with a name. For example, if you want to remember a formula in math, write it on paper in bold colours in large text, and as you say the formula, stare at it and repeat it a few times then close your eyes and see it in your mind and say it again. The job is now done. The next day in an exam, if you want to know the formula, just ask yourself, "What is that formula?" If it doesn't come straight away, then close your eyes and try and picture it then ask the question again. If it still hasn't arrived, just go on with the rest of the exam and forget about it. Just like Ralph's name, be confident. The formula will arrive very shortly.

This time, instead of waiting three days for Ralph's name, because you quickly studied just before the exam which is sometimes called cramming, the formula will arrive in seconds. Remember the brain processes information last in, first out. Be careful. Do not say, "Oh, no, I can't remember that formula," because the brain will think, "OK, you can't remember."

Third example is you have lost your keys. Just ask your brain where your keys are. The reason you lost your keys was because your mind was miles away when you placed them somewhere. If you never want to lose your keys again, watch the keys land on the table next time you throw them there. When your eyes see them land, the brain will process that image and you will soon know where the keys are after you ask your brain the question.

Fourth example is how many times when you have been introduced to someone you have forgotten his name within ten seconds. The reason this happened is, as you were shaking his hand during the introduction, your brain was summing him up and forming an opinion. This is very common, our need to make a quick assessment when meeting someone. Everyone does it. The brain prioritised the assessment as more important than remembering the name. If you want to remember his name, try to make no judgement as you meet him, and as he says his name, repeat it as you say, "Pleased to meet you," while looking at his face. Looking at his face and saying his name at the same time will do the job. After that is done, say his name a few times to yourself, then if you need to form an opinion now at least you have completed the correct introduction. Now if you forget the name a few minutes later, then just ask your brain while picturing his face in your mind. If you completed your introduction correctly, the name will soon come back to you. And it is very important to stop saying, "I can never remember names," because your brain will also help you to not remember.

There is a lot of information and examples on how the brain works. I could fill a book on it, but I have told you this much so you can start to build that new positive superhighway in your brain. Part of building up that positive superhighway is learning the difference between the conscious thinking brain and the subconscious mind. You must know that everything you think and everything that you see and everything that you say and do will leave an effect on your subconscious mind. The first you will know about it is when you are feeling anxiety and you wonder, *Why?* That will be your subconscious mind ticking away without you even knowing. For example, I'll share some negative language to avoid like. I can never remember names, that activity scares me, I always mess things up, I'm too dumb for that, I was never any good at that, I'm useless when it comes to that. All these sayings are put downs and if you say them regularly your brain will hold you back and keep you down. But your brain is only doing it because you keep reinforcing it so no more put downs of yourself and also of your fellow human beings. Putting down other people is usually done to reinforce your own insecurities.

Using positive language will improve your opinion of yourself and instil confidence in you and in your fellow human beings and also in life and you need confidence to rise above panic attacks. That is why we must build that positive superhighway in our brain, so we can train our conscious mind to accept and seek positive information and TRUST it so the next emotion we feel will be a smile instead of anxiety.

The Conscious Mind and the More Important Subconscious Mind

The Conscious Mind

I have always known that I have a conscious mind; I have known that if I think of something, then I do it that I am doing it consciously. But what I did not know was that everything that I do, see, think, or say is recorded in my brain, and my subconscious has a lifetime of access to it. Just like the example of remembering Ralph's name, it came three days later even though your conscious thinking mind was involved in another activity. Your busy, highly intelligent, subconscious mind was somewhere else delving into your past. Or you are about to participate in an activity in which you are continually saying I always mess things up and you are more nervous than you should be and you wonder Why.

These are perfect examples of why the subconscious mind is so important in explaining anxiety and fear. You may be involved in an activity and wondering why you are feeling anxiety, but deep in your mind, your subconscious is involved with a memory from many years ago, possibly as far back as your youth or remembering constant negative language that you use to describe yourself, and you have no idea what is going on. That experience from the past will have similarities with an event coming up in the near future. That is why I was convinced that the problems to my over active anxiety and fear were deep rooted in my subconscious youth to the over-proportional punishment and fear I experienced as a child and to my constant negative language and labels that I attached to myself since those times. I am not talking about everyday problems that give you genuine concerns. I am talking about minor problems that give you disproportional fear and anxiety. So when it comes to the conscious mind and our daily activities, we have to understand that what we are doing consciously could be effected by our subconscious mind, therefore affecting our future anxiety and confidence.

The Subconscious Mind

Until I had panic attacks, I did not even know what a subconscious mind was. I was reading books before my two trips to the psychologist, and the books constantly talked about the subconscious mind. I had to look it up in my dictionary, and it said, "Happening without one's awareness." It took me a little while to get my head around that meaning. I thought, *I have been aware of everything I have done.* What I didn't know is your mind is a constant thinking machine. The easiest way to explain it is when you are asleep and you are dreaming. Even when you are sleeping your body is still active like your heart beating your stomach is still digesting your vital organs are still filtering and your brain is still working in your subconscious mind. That's one example of your subconscious mind. And for me, that is all I knew. I did not know that it has many other functions.

In fact, the subconscious mind is so complicated that thousands of doctors and scientist have studied it, and they are still making discoveries. And there is probably more that is undiscovered that has been discovered. So I will not pretend to be an expert on the subconscious mind. I will only refer to my subconscious mind and what I have been told about it and what I have learnt about it.

The things that I have learnt about my subconscious are best described to you in examples. All these are typical examples of what has happened to me.

All my life, I have had nightmares, usually violent ones. This is happening while I am asleep. That is one example. Even while you are asleep, your subconscious mind is active. I later discovered that all the violence that I saw through the day came back to me at night in my dreams. I believe my nightmares were a message from my body to stop watching violence on TV.

A second example is that someone has asked me for help and I say, "Yes, no problem." And then seconds later, I get a hot flush of discomfort. That is an example of my mouth being operated by my in the now brain and saying one thing, but my in the past subconscious is not agreeing and sending me a physical emotion of discomfort. Although I may have agreed to help, my subconscious mind remembers that I do not really have time to spare because my schedule is full. Or it remembers the emotional pain the last time I was involved in a similar situation. This shows me that my past and future subconscious mind and my in the now brain which operates my mouth don't always agree.

Another example is if you are continually saying I hate my job. Then you regularly wake up feeling ill in the mornings because you keep saying I hate my job, while you are asleep your subconscious mind is still working to reinforce your negative language about your job. And if you hate something your brain will tell you in your conscious waking hours then your subconscious brain will take over in your sleeping hours. And the reason this happens is because you are continually reinforcing it in your negative brain network. And your ever obedient brain is only helping to reinforce your belief in the hate for your job even in your sleep because you unknowingly keep saying it.

Another example, I am sitting in a chair and watching television, something total harmless, but I am feeling flushed with heat. My heart is racing faster than normal, and I feel I'd better go to the bathroom now. This example shows that, although I was watching television in the now, my subconscious is not interested in television but is concerned with a big event next week, which I was not thinking about. Even when I wake up in the morning feeling sick in the stomach, which I have done most of my life, I know that all night long my subconscious was giving me nightmares and was worried about the next day's events.

As I have been working on easing my subconscious mind through not watching violence on television, my dreams have been much more pleasant. I know this because I no longer wake up feeling ill.

A subconscious which is not at ease with your body will let your body know with an emotion. With me, the emotion is always a sick feeling in the stomach along with a raise in temperature and a faster heartbeat. Perhaps other people get headaches or other symptoms. In fact, when I was young I remember my mother taking me to the doctor's regularly with upset stomach and nausea. All my adult life, I just lived with it. I thought it was a normal part of life. Now I rarely have an upset stomach these days, but when it is upset, I immediately think what is on my agenda. And I usually get an answer. At that point, I accept my anxiety, tell myself that everything will work out, and just TRUST life. And then I smile. I talk to my brain, saying, "My 'little mate' is sending me a message. Can you help him settle down and put him at ease?" My little mate is my subconscious mind.

So I know my brain gives me everything I ask for and relief has never been that far away. Then I ask my brain. An answer always comes to me, and then I start to deal with it with correct, positive thinking.

THE CONSCIOUS MIND
verses
THE SUBCONSCIOUS MIND

Earlier in the second chapter I mentioned my own discovery and I said that I would explain it later. I will explain my belief of my own subconscious mind and my conscious mind. I say my own because I have no scientific proof that this is going on in your head. But in my head I know and believe that is definitely going on so these examples are of me. Then you can make your own mind up about it and see if it is applicable to you.

We have all heard the sayings "I am always arguing with myself" or "I can't live with myself". And this is usually said by people who are experiencing some mental difficulty. And when you are having panic attacks you are definitely experiencing mental difficulty. The term "Myself" is you and your in the now thinking living brain. And the argument is with your "subconscious mind" which lives in the past and the future. I believe and know this to be true in my own experience from the knowledge that I have gained of my own brain.

Have you seen those old movies and cartoons where a person is arguing with themselves and an angel appears on one shoulder and a devil appears on the other shoulder. The angel is saying DO IT and the devil is saying DON'T DO IT and that person is arguing with themself. The angel can be compared to your positive in the now brain, the devil can be compared to your past and future negative subconscious mind.

An example you are a person suffering panic attacks and you have to do something simple like go shopping. But the thought of going shopping gives you anxiety and you are afraid that you might have a panic attack in public. Your positive in the now brain is saying GO IT WILL BE OK DO NOT BE AFFRAID you know shopping is harmless and your positive in the now brain is telling you that. However at the time your more powerful negative subconscious is saying DO NOT GO YOU WILL MAKE A FOOL OF YOURSELF. And then there is a war in your head which makes your body feel sick and nervous. This was my own experience during the panic attacks my confidence was so low that I struggled for a short time even to go shopping.

And now I know why, your positive language comes from your positive network and your negative doubt comes from your negative network. And if your negative network is far superior in size than your positive network then you will struggle with panic and anxiety. But your subconscious mind need not be compared to a devil. It could be compared to a struggling child who needs help and confidence and love and care, that struggling child is probably you as a kid. And instead of an angel the other image could be you as a confident leader giving that struggling kid encouragement love and understanding that he always deserved. Then your frightened subconscious will stop fighting and receive the love and encouragement that it has always been longing from you. As long as your subconscious mind and brain are moving in the same direction there will be no more arguments in your head. Although they are two separate identities and always will be they have become one in their direction and the tug of war between them is over. There may still be some difficulty because your subconscious still has doubts but it will gain in confidence as it is encouraged and succeeds. And some years later your life will be so good you may even want to write a book about it. It is easy to train an in the now brain just by simply believing and saying positive words. But a subconscious needs to be guided and encouraged eventually you will have a more confident and positive subconscious and your proof will be less anxiety and less fear. But even a positive subconscious will have some doubt occasionally and that is when you the confident leader and your brain will give it positive encouragement to help it through the difficulty as one. And the positive results will snowball and you will continue to grow and love your life.

That is my description of the discovery I made of the war in my head. And my subconscious and my conscious having separate identities and living in my head. And then becoming one in their direction and ending their tug of war in my head that contributed to my recovery from panic attacks. I do not know if it agrees with modern psychology because I worked it out for myself but it agrees with what I believe about my own brain and what you believe in comes true to you.

Why Panic Attacks Happened to Me
Those Early Years Had Left Their Mark

Why did panic attacks happen to me? Well, after receiving professional advice and researching all the books and online information, I learnt that a few factors brought them about. Firstly, I now know that those early years are the most influential on your brain and particularly your subconscious mind. Now looking back, I can see how my young brain reacted to fear and how it affected my vulnerable subconscious. Then as I grew older, I did not drop the fearful habits of my youth, therefore continually building that negative network in my brain. Now I see and feel the connection of a vulnerable, youthful subconscious and my constant negative language in my adult life.

I think most children grow up and break many of their fearful habits, as I did, but in my case, I never broke the old memories and language which caused them. I remember watching a scary movie when I was thirteen. It took me a few weeks to get over it; it really did scare me. I saw that same movie again when I was eighteen, and I actually laughed at it and wondered how I could have been so scared as a kid. But as a kid, you are affected more by fear. If I had adopted the same attitude to my life as I did to that movie and laughed at the things that scared me when I was a kid, there would not have been panic attacks as I grew older. But instead, I resented my over-disciplined and overworked youth and thought about it many times with anger, resentment, and bitterness and sometimes even revenge.

It was my constant negative thinking of my youth that was a large contributor to the panic attacks and my constant use of negative language as an adult which I attached to those memories. Secondly, the human body and the human brain have evolved into a life survival machine. Part of survival in the ancient and modern world is a respect for fear. Evolution has told our brains to be careful, and there is a modern term called "fight or flight" where our human instinct or our brain will prepare us to fight or prepare us to run.

So as an infant, you are already born with an internal protection mechanism which is fear based, but it is there to protect you. Then as a young child, like most others, I was exposed to fear for different reasons. Fear was used to protect me, things like, "Don't do this or that" or "Don't go there because you will be hurt." Fear was used to punish me: "If you don't do this or if you go there, you will be punished." Fear was used to educate me. "Hell is a very bad place and if you are bad you will go there. And if you don't pay attention and do as I say, you will be punished." And examples of history where people didn't do as they were told and the punishment they received. Fear was used to inform me like the daily news of bad things that were happening around the world. Fear was used to entertain me like a scary movie or a scary story.

So fear was alive and well in me when I was young and developing, and these were the most influential years of my life. As a young child, I would have received some love and praise also, but they are not the things that I remember with my genetically inbuilt protection system of fight or flight. And with the use of fear in my daily life, the seed of fear was well and truly planted in me at a very young age. That seed grew into a negative snowball, which kept growing and growing.

Then as I started to develop into my middle teens, I was rebelling against punishment and I started to fight. Psychologists will tell you that from infancy to your middle teens are the most influential years of your life, and a large part of your character is formed by then. As I grew from my middle teens to adulthood, my brain was making up its own mind about fear and I began to dispel them as adults do. But my subconscious was living in my youth because that is where most of my fearful thinking was. So I consider myself to be like most children who take the flight option in those very influential years. While all this was happening, the negative snowball in my brain kept growing, building and strengthening the negative network.

The Negative Snowball Effect That Led to My Panic Attacks

So there was an inbuilt survival system the seed of fear negative language and thoughts that were planted in me when I was young. These factors are extremely common in many young children, but not all young children will grow up to have panic attacks. But I have seen figures that say a large percentage of people will have a panic attack in their lifetime. For many people, that one panic attack will become just a bad experience, but there will be others like me where one panic attack snowballs into another one and then again and again. The next thing that you know, you have lost all your confidence and walking out the front door leads to your next panic attack.

I grew up to have panic attacks and others didn't because my negative thoughts and language were trapped in my youth, and I took the negative seed of fear and I nourished it. I took a seed and turned it into a giant negative snowball, which had created a negative superhighway in my brain, which in turn was devouring what was left of my redundant positive thinking circuitry. Now that my early years of development had passed, I had the responsibility of my own well-being. As a young child, I resented the verbal and physical punishment that I received and was not able to question it. But as an adult, if someone said or treated me in that fashion, I would stand and fight and I did.

The thing is, as an adult I was mostly treated with respect there were times I had to stand up to someone who threatened me with violence or insulting remarks but now I deal with these things much differently.

In my case, panic attacks were inevitable. Looking back now with a sound mind, the answer is clear to me. I was relentless with my own self-punishment, which grew my negative snowball. I no longer had adults to punish me, so I did it to myself. From age sixteen to age fifty, I used all the verbal insults I received as a child and multiplied them many times over.

How come I treat everyone else with patience and respect, but I had no patience and respect for myself? I would verbally abuse myself. I would fight with myself. I used fear to motivate myself. When my life was running along smoothly, I lived with myself but rarely gave myself any credit—only abuse when things went wrong, this is a replica of my youth which I now used on myself as an adult. This is why I believe I had the panic attacks. My negative network had taken over. In the end, there could be no positive result. It could have been worse. Perhaps if I was not as healthy or physically as strong as I am, I could have given myself a heart attack. Who knows what might have happened? I consider myself lucky to have gotten away with just having the panic attacks.

How My Brain Works, and Be Careful What You Ask For

In this next section of the book, I will explain how my brain has worked and how it has affected me. I will give some examples. I am writing these from a viewpoint that I am getting to know my brain pretty well, and from experience all the pieces of the puzzle of life are falling into place. The answers just keep coming to me.

My life demands that I think and that I have thoughts. That is the way it is. To be able to clear the mind for short periods of time is an exercise that I am continually practising, and it is getting better. I am able to clear my mind for short periods of time, particularly when I want to fall asleep. But from the moment that I wake up in the morning, if there is something to do within one minute or even seconds of waking up, my mind is thinking and the restful peace has disappeared. Now this is not a bad thing, because in the real world, my life must go on and it does not matter what I am doing on that day. My subconscious that was working during my sleep has now passed the baton over to my waking brain and says, "Over to you mate. We have work to do."

I know this for a fact only through my experience. I have no scientific proof that it happens, but it's my brain and I know it happens. So it does not matter what my agenda is on that day. It may be work, a meeting, a job, a trip, a game of golf, family matters, or even writing this book. Within seconds of waking up, I get an appropriate emotion to the task at hand. I will feel the need to get out of bed and start my preparation. Usually the first thing is off to the bathroom and then a cup of tea and so on.

My Common Mistake

Now the big mistake and the most common mistake that I used to make was when I first woke up, in the pre-panic days, within seconds I would misread the emotion in my body and tap into my negative network by saying, "I feel dreadful." I would begin a negative snowball, and the rest is history. For me, that emotion that my body receives from my brain in the morning does not sometimes feel good, particularly if there is something very important on the calendar.

But in the world of my daily life, there is usually something to be done and in the morning, I no longer misread that emotion. A typical morning now is within seconds of waking up, I feel my tummy is not right but the difference now is I say, "Yes, mate, I've got the message. Let's get things happening." I do not kid myself that I feel well if I do not feel well. I just say, "OK, mate, I understand. Let's get going." I begin a positive snowball and work on turning that feeling around.

Now back to that big mistake of misreading that initial emotion within seconds of waking up. It is not pleasant waking up with a mildly upset stomach, but that is all it is: mildly upset. My huge mistake was to wake up and say to myself within seconds, "I feel dreadful." But it wasn't dreadful; it was just uncomfortable. Remember what I said earlier: if my brain is capable of delivering something, it will do it so the negative snowball got off to a flying start. So within seconds, I would feel worse and bad thoughts equal bad feelings so I just unknowingly put my negative snowball into high gear.

As I began to feel worse, I would start thinking that my task for the day would be a lot tougher than it should be. Then my brain would pick up on my bad thoughts with more bad feelings, and that mildly upset stomach is now a very upset stomach. The next thought would be, *I don't know if I can make it. I feel so sick.* Then my brain would start its defence mode by giving me thoughts of, *You better not go, Paul. What if you get sick and make a fool of yourself?* The war in my head had begun. It usually got even worse from there. My negative snowball was well and truly building from anywhere between difficulty and despair to panic, but at that time I did not know any better. That was my life then.

Sometimes your own negative commentary of saying things like "I don't feel well" turn to "I feel sick," then turn to "I feel dreadful," "I can't cope," and ultimately, "I'm not going." All these sayings could have been nipped in the bud at the beginning by saying, "Yes, I am feeling a bit off, and I accept it, but that's OK. I can cope." And now your subconscious mind and your brain are working together as one in a positive direction and the argument of doubt is over.

Now that I know how my brain works, I no longer make those simple mistakes that are so common with many people and I have ceased the constant negative language that led to feeling ill. So you see now I know that in that first instance in the morning, I now have the option to accept that very first emotion, which in my case is usually in my stomach on those important days, and I do accept it. And then with positivity and honesty start my positive snowball to help me get through that particular task of the day, but I keep it positive and honest.

If it is a very important occasion, that initial emotion in your tummy may be very upset, so do not try to kid yourself by saying things like, "No worries, mate. This will be a breeze. I feel great." Although it is far better than negative self-talk, I found that it would help me get through the day, even though that entire day I would struggled with the war in my head.

I found that my brain responded to positive self-talk with honesty, which helped build my confidence as I woke up not feeling well uniting my brain as one. I acknowledged it and accepted it, as there was any sign of relief in my stomach. As I got moving, it would help bring that little smile of, "Yes, it's getting better," and my positive snowball would begin growing—sometimes to the point of comfort, ease, or even confidence. Sometimes that initial sick feeling in the morning would lead to a beaming smile and confidence and an attitude of "Whatever happens next does not matter. I have already won." And the victory was over those old negative ways of the past you must always TRUST.

Later in the book, in the chapter dealing with panic attacks, we will go through the entire process from the time you wake up in the morning dealing with anxiety that leads to panic attacks.

So now I have tried to explain how my brain works, and I think that others may be making the same mistakes I once did with negative language that divides the brain and continues the war.

A Discovery That Led to Another Turning Point

At this stage of my recovery, I had realised the important connection between the subconscious and the conscious mind, but this next example explains how big this connection is. And after making this discovery, there was no turning back to my old negative ways.

Engineering has been my life. One night I was watching an engineering program on television. They spoke about the fine tolerances of the machinery in metric measurements. In my sleep, my brain completed a complex mathematical conversion from metric measurements to imperial measurements, and then in the middle of the night I woke up with an imperial measurement in my head accurate to thousandths of an inch it was the same conversion that I used regularly with a calculator thirty years ago. I was amazed that this could be done in my sleep and that my brain still remembered the formula. Then two weeks later, I realised the enormity of it. I thought to myself, *My brain just wants to please me. Everything that I ask for that it can deliver, it will.* Many times when I saw people do mathematical equations before my New Age thinking days, I would say I would like to be that smart, and now I was—even in my sleep. At this point, I thought, *All those years when I abused myself and my brain by calling it names, when all my brain wanted to do was give me what I was asking for*

A mistreated brain can be likened to a mistreated dog that has been surrendered to the pound because his owner is unable to control it because he thinks it has become aggressive and unmanageable. Then a new owner rescues him from the pound then teaches and trains him correctly and the dog becomes the love of his new owner's lives. This was our experience with our third Dalmatian we renamed him Rocco and after rescuing him from the pound and retraining him, he became the love of our lives. Rocco also had to learn how to love after being mistreated he had a problem with trust which he turned around to being so loyal and loving just like your brain will be. Apart from my wife my brain is the new love of my life.

Remember earlier in the book how we recalled Ralph's name even though it had been ten years since we had seen him. Our brain remembered and wanted to help us and recalled Ralph's name so if you have been calling yourself idiot and stupid then your brain also remembers; this example cannot be argued with it proves itself. Your brain was designed to help you not hinder you like some people may think. Remember when I said earlier in the book that your brain does not forget that you asked a question only you forget that you asked a question. Your brain also does not forget that you insulted it by calling it stupid only you forget that you insulted it.

Just imagine how you would feel if you had a faithful friend whose lifetime job it was to give you everything he was capable of, but you abused that friend and called him names. You would feel dreadful. Well, that is how I felt. That friend was my brain.

Now what I am about to say is what I think is one of the most significant turning points in my recovery: I humbly apologised to my brain. And it was genuine and sincere.

You may be thinking I am crazy or you might agree with me, but my apology went like this: "My beautiful brain, I did not know that all those years that I abused myself that I was damaging you. I promise to never abuse you ever again. Please forgive me for my past mistakes. I would never treat anyone like I treated you. From now on I will only give you good thoughts and kind words and love, which you have always deserved."

Although at this point I had already made big improvements and had not verbally abused myself for some time, I really do believe that the apology to my brain and the pledge to never abuse it again and only give it good thoughts and love greatly accelerated and reinforced my recovery by uniting me as one. Now my newfound respect and knowledge of how my brain works and the retraining of my brain helped me understand and deal much better with fear and anxiety.

This discovery I worked out for myself so I have no scientific proof for it other than my example.

CHAPTER 5

Fear and Anxiety

Fear, Then Anxiety, Then Panic

In my case, it was important to understand the connection of fear then anxiety then panic. An example was if I had fear and I was afraid of something, it would give me anxiety and I would know why I had anxiety this example is obvious. A less obvious example is if I was occupied with an activity but my subconscious mind had fear, then I would have anxiety but I would not know why I was feeling ill. Anxiety is the first emotion of fear, whether your are consciously thinking of it or you are unaware and your subconscious is dwelling on it while you are occupied doing other things. Once you are aware of the anxiety and then trace it back to the cause, it can be dealt with.

At this stage, if the fear is not dealt with correctly and positively, then the fear will aggravate the anxiety and make the anxiety worse, which in turn will make the fear even worse. Now this is the beginning of a panic attack. Once the fear reaches panic proportions, the anxiety level will rise to the point of overwhelming you. The heart can beat so fast and the body can get so hot that you will struggle to regain your composure. If you come to your senses and snap of out your negative snowball and realise what is happening, you can avoid a panic attack. But if you remain in the negative snowball, the anxiety and the fear and the panic will grow off each other, and then there is a panic attack. I found this out the hard way. It was a typical pattern that I followed with anxiety that led to panic attacks.

Even anxiety can be looked at positively. Anxiety can be your early warning system to point to your fear and unite your brain then address the fear positively. We would all prefer not to have anxiety, but anxiety happens. So instead of letting the ill feeling of anxiety linger on endlessly, use it as a warning system to engage your positive snowball and address the cause of the anxiety, which will be fear, either conscious fear or subconscious fear.

My own experience agrees strongly with what I have read in books and what I have had explained to me by professionals. You cannot eliminate fear; fear comes before anxiety. To feel anxious, firstly there has to be a fear of something. If you are aware of what is causing you fear, you are one step ahead and have some chance of addressing it. If you are feeling anxious and do not know why perhaps you may misinterpret your anxiety as being ill, then you will probably be off to the doctor to look for a cure. The doctor's job is made so much more difficult if you only tell him about your upset tummy and your lack of appetite and not your other problems.

I feel that every day in my new direction in life, I am becoming less fearful of the things that gave me panic attacks, but I have fifty years of fearful habits to break. By the way, that direction in life that I talk about is peace in my own body, but more on peace later.

After two years in my new direction and all the good advice and the things I worked out for myself, my panic attacks have gone. But I do on occasions suffer some anxiety and usually for insignificant reasons. Then I accept my feelings, address them, and usually smile, thinking the old me is trying to sneak back in. But the old negative me is gone forever. I know that things in the future will probably give me genuine concern and whatever they may be I will address them at the time. But fear for the minor details of everyday life is a thing of the past.

Fear and the Value of Fear

Having asked myself the question to better understand fear and why my reaction to fear led to anxiety and panic attacks, it didn't take long for answers to start coming my way. Panic and anxiety come from fear. I listed all the things that I was afraid of on a piece of paper and examined them. It took some honesty on my behalf. I had to be honest with myself to truly get the answers, because on the outside it looked like that I had no fear, but I had no problems on the outside. My problems were on the inside, and on the inside I had anxiety and fear.

The answers came thick and fast, then I placed my fears in the order of their intensity and how much they affected me. I listed them on paper, then I addressed my fears to deal with them, and this helped me greatly. I will start with the fear that affected me the least, which was the fear of pain, and I will end with the fear that had the greatest effect on me, which was the fear of embarrassment.

1. **The fear of pain**. As a young child, I was greatly afraid of pain because being smacked or caned hurt, but the more smacks and the more pain that came my way and the older I became, I actually got used to pain. At home, I wasn't allowed to show pain: the typical stuff like don't you cry or you will get more of the same. At school, it did not matter how many cuts of the cane that I received, although it hurt I just stood there with zero emotion then walked away like it never happened. I went from a frightened nine year old to a fifteen year old who began rebelling against over punishment, on occasions I laughed at the brothers when I received the cane and received even greater punishment because of it. I knew it would make things worse but it was my way of trying to save face. Many times a brother would cane me without any emotion or insult and I accepted it they were just doing their job, and I could respect that. But on occasions when the cane came with insults and humiliation as I grew older and became more confident I would laugh in their face which made things worse. By the time I was fifteen like many young kids I had been involved with different self defence courses and pain was now something that I accepted.

   So now living an average, everyday life in suburbia, I am sensible and there is little reason to be afraid of pain.

2. **The fear of things not being good.** Whatever I was involved in, I would say, "All that I want is that it turns out to be good." It didn't matter if it was a day out or a project or work and particularly a holiday. All I wanted was that it turned out to be good. And I realise this was a contributor to my anxiety; before any event, I wanted it to be good. Now at my age, I have good reasons to put this fear away. Things have always turned out to be good. I have learnt acceptance and my attitude now is that "It will be whatever it will be." I can take a great deal of comfort in that, because with hindsight, things have always been good to me, even my failures, which were hard to accept at the time. They have always turned out to lead to better things, which have contributed to a better life, so my anxiety for the need for things to be good is very low, and I am always working on my acceptance.

3. **The fear of failure.** This was a tough fear before I discovered I was very intelligent. When I believe that I am not smart because I have been told that by educated adults whenever I sat for any exam, I was struggling with my failure anxiety. My attitude was I would take 51 percent because I was stupid, but exams were not the only anxiety. There was the anxiety of failing and how I was going to explain it, and it gave me great stress at the time. But then there was my introduction to New Age thinking, which led me to discover that I am highly intelligent. Everyone is highly intelligent as you will also discover. After that, it was no longer a question of if I would pass but more a question of by how far I could pass, and would I get 100 percent? I am no longer interested in going back to technical college to achieve knowledge; my direction of knowledge now is to pursue peace and learn how to attract it to me, and to learn more ways of how to love life. So my anxiety of failure now is almost non-existent. How can I fail when all that I now ask for is to learn how to love life?

4. **The fear of not being accepted and fear of not fitting in.** This is another fear where hindsight and acceptance have been able to reduce this fear to almost zero. This fear of not being accepted

was greater when I was young. As a youth, we all called each other names because we didn't know any better, and then we formed groups where we are accepted and we hung out with like-minded kids. As a youth, I didn't like being called names by other kids my own age and it got me into a lot of trouble. But kids stop calling each other names when they are old enough to know better. When I began working, I noticed that name-calling among adults was almost non-existent and it was the adults who had not fully grown up yet that persisted in name-calling. Now at this stage of my life, I have met people from all walks of life and nationalities, religions, wealth, and education and I have not once been made to feel inferior by a fair minded adult. So my experience, hindsight, and acceptance have reduced this fear of not being accepted to almost nil.

5. **The fear of God and of not going to heaven.** I was educated at a Catholic school to have a healthy fear of God, and I did fear God, but I think my fear of dying and not going to heaven was even greater. I don't think like that anymore all my faith now revolves around love. I need my faith to instil love in me and not fear. I will explain this further later in the book.

6. **My greatest fear is the fear of embarrassment.** I believe that the fear of embarrassment was the greatest fear that contributed to my past anxiety and panic attacks. So many times growing up, I heard, "You will embarrass the family name," if I did not do exactly as my parents instructed. At school, punishment often came with embarrassment and insults, and calling each other names at school came with a lot of embarrassment, particularly when they became racial in nature. As an adult, I soon learnt that I would not embarrass anyone because I didn't like being embarrassed. As an adult, I found that if I broke something, I could fix it, and if I failed something, I could try again then pass it. And I found out that pain is only short lived, but embarrassment, well, it was the hardest to live with. And it lingers in your subconscious memory. Even heaven and hell were sometime in the future, but

embarrassment was right now. All my life, when I engaged in anything and felt the greatest anxiety, it wasn't my fear of pain, failure, or things not being good. It was if I embarrassed myself by looking foolish and had to live with embarrassment and criticism and I can see that connection to my youth.

I am dealing with this one and I have a lot of work to do on it. I have in some respect largely overcome it and I had to go back to my youth and rewrite some memories. I say to myself that it is better to have a go and fail even if I do look a little bit silly than not to have a go at all and give in to anxiety. I have given myself room to move on this too by allowing things to go wrong, because it happens and by not trying to look perfect at what I am doing and also by being able to have a little chuckle at my own expense. Even writing this book is testing me. The fear of writing something that is laughed at does have an effect on me, but as I just said, at least I had a go.

So I have made a lot of progress on this fear, but it is the hardest one to overcome. I could tell myself that I beat this fear, but next time I feel anxious it will probably be the culprit. But I have done a lot of work on it, and the anxiety of looking stupid is largely gone. It was the fear of embarrassment that ignited the greatest war in my head and now that I am aware of it things are on the mend I know that because my anxiety is vastly reduced. But to put my hand on my heart and say it doesn't bother me would be false. I think that is only human nature.

So having knowledge of these fears and addressing them the way I have has greatly reduced my anxiety and has not allowed it to go to a panic stage. I also stopped the negative language that led up to these fears, the negative language that was affecting my subconscious and dividing my head without my knowledge or intension. There may be an answer that eliminates fear and anxiety, but I haven't found it and I do not want to eliminate fear. I only want to keep it in proportion. If there is a time for a little concern, then that's what I want: a little concern. I do not want to blow it out of all proportion and turn it into panic.

These values of fear are something that I worked out for myself, with all the help I had and gaining knowledge of how my brain works. These values of fear plus the evolution of flight or fight and my constant negative language, I believe, are close to the truth of my anxiety and panic. By understanding them, it will help me deal with them but it cannot help me eliminate them.

If I was to say that I eliminated all these fears, I would be holding myself up to a standard that I could not live up to. I would be preaching one thing, but inside, where my peace lives, I would be feeling something else. I definitely have been able to reduce them to a point where they are acceptable to me, and now that I know what causes them, I totally believe I will be able to control my anxiety to a more comfortable level.

Anxiety Hangover

Anxiety hangover is something that I discovered for myself, which took some understanding. I can remember participating in events that caused me to have anxiety, and usually after the event there would be some relief that it was over. But total relief did not happen the next day. I usually felt off, but not as bad as the previous day. And then the panic attacks happened.

In those initial panic-attack days, there was no relief. I felt dreadful all the time. Then when the panic subsided to anxiety, I wondered why I still felt ill after the event had passed. And the next day, there was no pressure, yet I still felt more ill than I should. Then the answers came to me: "too much anxiety leaves you with an anxiety hangover." It's just like too much alcohol leaves people with a hangover the next day. So I had to be patient some days. If I had suffered too much high anxiety, I had to accept the next day might not give me all the relief that I hoped for. I learnt that there was a recovery period after anxiety, and I learnt to accept it and not misread it as a problem. This helped me to understand why some achievements did not lead to instant relief. I still had to be patient and positive that the relief would be arriving.

Sometimes relief from anxiety takes even longer if your mental health is down, so this next topic is one to be avoided: complaining.

Complaining

All my life I had difficulty listening to people complaining, particularly when I was going through those difficult times of panic attacks. For me, listening to people complain about everyday life seems meaningless. And when I was suffering anxiety and panic, listening to people complaining caused me great stress and even greater anxiety.

I have always had an issue of not offending people. I would always put their need to complain and talk about their problems in life before my need of wanting to walk away or tell them to stop complaining. So I would politely listen and then feel drained when they finally walked away. Now most people are fine, but you will know the ones that I am talking about here: the ones who bail you up.

Avoid telling these people your problems and for one good reason. Not only do they like telling you their problems, they also like telling you other people's problems, people who you don't even know. Complaining and drama are their entertainment. That is how they pass the time of day. Once you have told them your problem, you have played into their hands. Now they have more gossip to pass onto the next person. Only tell your genuine problems to people you can trust or to professional people. All my life, when asked, "Hi, Paul, how are you?" I always answered, "Fine, thanks," even when I was feeling off.

On one occasion when I was suffering anxiety, one of those people who you want to avoid said hi then unloaded all their pain onto me. Twenty minutes later, that person walked away and her burden had been relieved. The problem was because I was too polite to tell that person that I had even bigger problems, I was now shouldering her burden plus my own. I was very ill for the rest of the day. And when you are having panic and anxiety and feel like I did on that day, terrible thoughts go through your head. Thoughts like "I can't take this anymore" and "Now I am in a state of depression." And when that happens, you need help.

So my message is if you are suffering from panic attacks, you will be more than likely in a poor mental state. Avoid talking to people who use complaining, tragedy, and gossip as their entertainment. And only talk to people you can trust or professional people about your situation.

CHAPTER 6

What Contributes to Anxiety

I have identified several elements that contributed to my old life of anxiety, and now that I have changed many of my old negative ways and habits, much more of my everyday anxiety has left me. These next reasons for anxiety are less obvious than the more common ones of complaining and negativity, so I would like to explain them and perhaps you may like to do the same. Not only has breaking these old habits led to lessening my anxiety, they have greatly improved my appreciation and my love of life.

Prejudging: Just Don't Do It

Prejudging also contributed to my old anxiety ways. At times, I did not even have to meet someone. If I saw people, I would automatically have an opinion of them based on their appearance. And I found it even worse when, before I met someone, if other people had given me negative information about that person, and it helped form an opinion for me.

When friends would say, "Avoid that person. He has a reputation for being mean," then my anxiety up to the next meeting would be even greater, because now I had information from reliable sources. But on these occasions, they were mostly wrong. I found that nine times out of ten, there was no problem. It was only their opinion and that we got along fine. So avoid prejudging and just trust people and trust life, and let the meeting go in whichever direction it goes. So that is another old habit broken of prejudging and a further reduction in my old collective of anxiety.

Opinions

Looking back now, I learnt that by having something as simple as an opinion added to my compulsive thinking, which added to my anxiety. Opinions which have the biggest effect and draw the most response are religion, politics, race, and class. When I learnt not to judge and not to criticise and to accept things the way they are, I learnt that my opinion just disappeared. If I'm asked my opinion, I usually dismiss the question by saying, "I don't know enough about the subject."

By having an opinion, I found that I usually had to take sides. Usually when you are asked an opinion, it is the beginning of a conversation on a particular subject. And when you take sides, you want to be right and you want your side to win. I found that my opinion was usually attached to my ego. And these things stirred my emotions, so when it comes to religion, politics, race, and class, to me they are fine. So many times opinions lead to serious debate or even arguments. The argument may not even be with someone else; the argument could be with yourself in your own head and having an opinion has ignited another war in there. And next thing you know, your subconscious is triggered and your subconscious is not at peace. Then another sleepless night is coming your way. So breaking another old habit by not having an opinion has also contributed to my peace and my acceptance by not getting involved.

My Exercise and Anxiety

When it comes to my own anxiety, I found exercise was a double-edged sword; it helped my anxiety at times, and it also caused me anxiety at times.

All my married life, until the last four years, we had large dogs which needed exercise. We had Dalmatians and they had so much energy. We walked them twice each day, morning and night. And we loved our dogs. Looking back, I see how owning dogs and exercising them and loving them helped disguise my anxiety without me even knowing it. When you have anxiety, the love that you have for your dogs helps divert attention from your own problems. After the panic attacks, I turned to walking as one of my diversions.

Apart from loving and walking dogs, I also had many activities which helped me divert my mind; at the time, I did not know that they were diversions. I had a bench with a barbell and weights for my muscles, and I had a few different punching bags and a skipping rope for my aerobics. I used those most of my life particularly when I was stressed, from my teenage years to age fifty-one.

Now I will get into how these activities helped and also hindered my anxiety. Until two years ago, I was a believer in "no pain, no gain." And how wrong I was with this opinion. Now I am a firm believer in "no fun, no gain."

During those panic days, I did not have the energy or the time to exercise, so there was a nine-month break from exercising. When life was getting back to normal, I got back to exercising. I had a routine which I still use, but I have toned it down immensely. I would exercise at home with weights on Monday and Tuesday then I would have Wednesday off, then exercise Thursday and Friday, then have the weekend off. And then I would do it all over again.

On my return to exercising and recovery from panic, I was waking up at 2 a.m. as I had done all of my life and was not able to get back to sleep so I would get up and exercise. Then I would be tired and get back to sleep around 3 or 4 a.m. This was becoming a regular habit, and I recognised it as a bad habit that I was going to break. It was also at the same time that I decided to break the habit of going to the bathroom at night.

It was around one year since the panic attacks and I was finally sleeping through the night without the need to get up. This was a major breakthrough for me. There were mornings when I woke up and my body was in peace, and it was a new and beautiful experience to me. But on mornings that were on my exercise schedule, there was no peace and I could feel anxiety from the moment I woke up. I could not keep still on these mornings. I would get up then I would push myself through my no-pain, no-gain attitude right through to the finish about forty minutes later. After this, I would say to myself, "I'm glad that is over." Then the next day I would go through it all over again.

By this time, I had asked myself and my brain to show me ways that led to a better life of less anxiety. Then one day I realised I didn't like my exercise and that my attitude of no pain, no gain and continually pushing myself is a masquerade. No pain, no gain is the common attitude and belief that world-class athletes use. It may serve them well, but I'm in my fifties and I just do not enjoy what I am doing. I can see how it is causing me to have anxiety instead of helping me deal with it. From now on, I am not going to give in to exercise. It has to be fun, and it has to be on my terms.

So then I came up with "no fun, no gain." I gave away all of my weights and barbells and I kept the exercise bench and two five-kilogram dumbbells. Now my exercise routine is much lighter and far easier and very enjoyable. I still do it four days per week 90 percent of the time, because if I am too busy or something else has used my energy on that day I don't bother with the exercise. My wife and I walk almost every day, depending on the weather and time, and as for my boxing equipment, I threw it out. I incorrectly used the boxing to deal with anger. So many times you get angry and someone says, "Well, get it off your chest." After all, hitting a punching bag is far better than fighting. But getting something off your chest and hitting a punching bag is still a diversion to me. I deal with stress and anger differently now which has also helped reduce my anxiety.

My Travel and Anxiety

I have noticed some friends, when asked how their holiday was, reply, "I got sick." At the time, I thought nothing of it, and this was a coincidence that they got sick just before or on that trip. A coincidence that I noticed had also happened to me, which I later discovered was a link between my travel and anxiety.

My first trip away after the panic attacks was a very tough one for me. It had been nine months since that first panic attack, and my confidence was high so I booked a holiday for a week away playing golf. In that last week leading up to the holiday, I could feel the anxiety building. Each day it got worse until finally it built up to panic-attack proportions. But this time, with my new positive mental approach, I was able to avoid the panic attacks, but the anxiety was difficult to deal with. Still, I managed. In the old days I would have thought that I had some illness and been off to the doctor. Every day on that trip away, I struggled with anxiety. In fact, I was relieved to arrive home. Again in the old days, I would have thought that I had contracted an illness just before the holiday and then some time after the holiday I recovered from that illness. This is not the case, now that I am aware of travel anxiety.

The next step for me was to find out why the anxiety gripped me so fiercely in those two weeks. So on my return; I contacted my hypnotherapist who is also a psychotherapist for an appointment. It had been about three months since my only other two visits.

We sat down and talked about it. She said, "There will be an answer in there, so let's find out what it is." So there I was totally relaxed while she kept asking me questions, she was right and eventually there were answers. Issues which caused me great anxiety and embarrassment when I was a kid which I had forgotten about and have dealt with since mentally. I went back to those incidences and told myself that was then and times have changed then I rewrote them mentally.

Until that hypnotherapy, I noticed that many times when I went away as an adult minor illnesses would happen, like the flu, an upset stomach, a rash, or headaches. And looking back now, I see they were all anxiety related. Now anxiety and travelling is nothing new; it is just that I thought my illness was a coincidence. So when I travelled, I would have a bag of medical supplies to accompany me.

In the last two years since that stressful trip, we have had some trips away for two weeks where we drove between two thousand and four thousand kilometres on each trip, and many one—or two-day road trips. With very little or no anxiety the bag of medical supplies came along, but it did not have to be used.

Anxious feelings around travel time are acceptable. So if they arise, I will accept them and deal with them as anxiety instead of as an illness. When it comes to travelling, if I am not feeling well, it will be anxiety that will be the first checkpoint.

Participating versus Competing

Learning to just participate instead of competing in my everyday life helped reduce my anxiety. If you think that sounds negative, that you should always compete to do your best, it will take a little explaining. If you want to read my theory about achieving your best results in your chosen field, whether it may be sport academics or work, then skip forward to the section titled "Learn to Love What You Are Doing."

Participating in life over competing in life is about reducing your anxiety and increasing your lifestyle. It is about enjoying and not competing it is about getting out and doing something instead of avoiding it. There are people who say they love competing, that it is the thrill of competition that they enjoy. Then this is not for them. I am aiming at people who suffer anxiety in their everyday activities.

I have been very competitive in my life. Most sports I tried I have been pretty good at, but not great at. But it did not stop me from trying hard. I always wanted to do my best, and when I didn't get the results, some frustration or anger crept in and that comes back as anxiety. I found that you keep trying, but frustration and anxiety hinder results.

When I discovered I did not enjoy my exercise because of my no-pain, no-gain attitude, I toned it down to suit my lifestyle, and then I began to enjoy it. I discovered that no-fun, no-gain worked for me. After adopting that attitude to all my other activities, more enjoyment and less anxiety came my way. I discovered that not pushing myself kept me exercising instead of giving exercising away. In my life, I also had to give golf away at times because I was not getting the results I wanted. So I adopted the same attitude to golf. Then one year later, not only was I enjoying my golf just like my exercise, I was also playing the best golf of my golfing career. In golf you cannot always have a good score but you can always have a good time if you choose enjoyment over results.

Because I refused to let my competitive nature interfere with my enjoyment, the results of enjoyment were easy to achieve. Now I chose enjoyment over my need for good results or winning. Enjoyment is up to you. Enjoyment is a choice. Results are not a choice. Good results are something you want, but good results can cause anxiety if they are not coming your way. So when I thought about it, I was no longer competing. I was turning up to participate, and enjoyment was my reward for participating every time. I used sport as an example but it could be as simple as not competing for that parking spot in the shopping centre don't argue with someone and beep your horn at them and don't let your ego get involved just drive onto the next spot and walk the extra one hundred metres.

My life would have been poorer if I had given up exercising and golf because of anxiety. And now they add to my love of life, but they are not the only things that my new attitude has improved. They are just two examples.

Life can be so competitive if you let it, but now I still do everything that I used to do. But in my case, I choose fun and I don't compete. I participate. And participating in life is achievable to everyone of every age group. And if you participate and chose fun instead of competing for results, then less anxiety will be your reward and your longevity in that interest will be extended. In my case, better results came with more fun and less stress. So not only did learning to participate instead of competing help lower my anxiety, it also gave me a better quality of life.

CHAPTER 7

The Positive Snowball

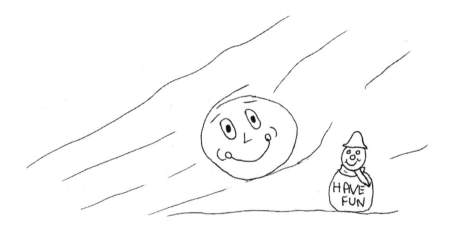

I mentioned earlier in the book about building that positive network in the brain called our positive snowball or superhighway. And I also mentioned that if you want something that your brain can deliver that you simply ask your brain and it will deliver it. And I also mentioned if you have a positive thought and you reinforce it with a positive emotion then it is reinforced in the positive network in your brain. So with these three bits of information, let me explain how I set about getting my positive snowball rolling, which is growing more positive and confident every day.

The centre of my positive snowball is the word *beautiful*, and everything that I see and that I think and that I do revolves around the word *beautiful*. I asked my brain to give me a smile whenever I say *beautiful*.

I asked my brain to catch my thoughts when I slipped into old habits of negativity, such as fearful negative thinking. After having success with this, I asked my brain to catch my thoughts when it slipped into old bad habits, such as criticizing, opinions, and prejudging. And it worked each time that my mind went into one of these old bad habits. My brain would bring it to my attention and at that point I would stop then smile and say, "Thank you, beautiful." Yes, I call my brain beautiful. It is the same word I used now to describe everything in my life. Of course, this is in my internal language. No one can hear it but me.

By doing this I believe that my subconscious and my conscious minds were now both heading in the same direction and snowballing together, instead of fighting and arguing in my head. And it was the word beautiful and acceptance of life and understanding of how each work that keeps them snowballing together.

At this stage, I was describing life and everything in life as beautiful, and each time I said that word in my internal language, it made me smile. In any average day in my internal language, I would say the word *beautiful* hundreds of times, and each time I smiled. In the days when I was coming out of anxiety or these days if I am experiencing anxiety, I would be saying the word *beautiful* in my internal language thousands of times per day until I rose above the anxiety. Now my positive snowball is unstoppable as it continues to build that positive network in my brain into a positive superhighway it only takes TRUST.

Strength and Confidence

After each episode of anxiety has passed, if you remain in your positive network in your brain, then as the positive network grows, your strength and confidence to deal with anxiety also grow. And each time you do this, it will become easier for you to deal with until you outgrow your old false fears. This sounds obvious and it is obvious, but it is not always the case. Some people will struggle greatly after each panic attack because they are still in their negative network. And their negative network will keep them trapped there. After all, it was your negative network that led to panic attacks.

So if you want to grow in confidence after each success against anxiety and panic, you must stay in your positive network and unite your brain as one. If each episode of anxiety is as powerful as the last one and you are not growing in confidence, then perhaps you are slipping back to negativity and letting that argument continue in your head. So as you make these gains over your old negative network and your anxiety eases, give yourself a little smile and encouragement to stay in your positive network and watch how you're confidence grows.

The Value of a Smile

HELLO   Hi

The value of a smile cannot be overlooked. I believe in the power of attraction, and I believe that smiling attracts good things to my life. I know smiling makes me feel better and smiling and the word *beautiful* are the centrepiece of my positive snowball. Whenever I say the word *beautiful* in my internal language, I automatically smile. All my life I have smiled; even in my old anxiety days, I used a smile to disguise how I was feeling. But these days, the smile is genuine and for the right reasons to show my appreciation for my beautiful life. When I was nineteen I saw a beautiful eighteen year old girl with a beautiful smile, four years later we were married and we have now celebrated our thirtieth wedding anniversary together.

I once heard of a book where a man with a serious illness cured himself with laughter. Well, genuine laughter begins with a smile. I don't think that the two can be separated. I know the brain can produce chemicals some feel unpleasant and some feel pleasant and help us to relax. And these pleasant chemicals, I figure, can only be in the positive network in our brain. So if laughing could help this gentleman's illness, I think smiling is almost laughing and I can smile all day long.

During my old panic-attack days, I just could not smile. I was not diagnosed with depression, but I am pretty sure I had it. So if you are struggling to smile, I know how you feel, but smiling is a good turning point to begin your new positive life.

The Power of an Image

Imagery is a powerful tool; in the days when I was struggling with panic and anxiety, books and professional advice were pointing to imagery to help ease anxiety. There were many suggestions picturing yourself in beautiful places, picturing yourself triumphing over adversity, and picturing your troubles floating away with the clouds. Picturing images was useful to me. At first, I was picturing myself conquering panic attacks. And then I discovered the importance of my affirmations where I kept them honest to my situation. Like "I am struggling now, but I know it will get better."

So all my mental imagery became relevant to my struggle at the time, then all my mental imagery was of me with only a little smile on my face. In my mental imagery, I conquered nothing other than achieving a small smile. When I began to discover the importance of my youth and the connection with my anxiety and panic, I added an image of me as a child with a smile on my face. Just like with my affirmations where I did not set lofty goals in my mental imagery, my goal was to smile.

When times were tough coming out of panic attacks and anxiety, I was struggling because of commitments I had to attend. In those early anxiety days, even if those commitments were a trip to the shopping centre or a bus ride into the city, I would need all my positive skills just to go through with it. As I was going into my positive self-talk and encouraging myself to persevere, my imagery was of me with a smile of contentment.

When things were tough, I continued picturing my smile, and then a genuine smile did appear on my face. My persistence with imagery which led me to achieving 100 percent for many of my exams of the past was now delivering me a genuine smile. And that smile and the word *beautiful* became the centre of my positive snowball.

When I was taught to retain information to pass exams, imagery was part of the process. You look at something then stare at it while saying it, then you close your eyes, see it in your mind, and say it while holding that mental image. I know this works; my exam marks proved it.

An Exercise in Imagery

Now that I have explained imagery and earlier we discussed the brain and the importance of faith and trust in recovery from panic attacks. I believe that faith and trust are the same thing so I would like to use the word "trust" in an exercise. This exercise is aimed at helping you block doubtful thoughts and images when they enter your head. Now you must learn to trust life all those times people have said negative things about life like life sucks or life is out to get you. You must not believe these things you must believe that life is beautiful.

Now in a quiet place where there is no disruption write the word TRUST on a piece of paper in bold colour in capital letters. Now stare at the word TRUST and say the word while staring at it. Now close your eyes and see the word TRUST and while seeing it in your mind say the word TRUST.

Now look at the word again on paper and this time add a small smile while seeing the word TRUST. Now close your eyes with a little smile on your face see the word TRUST in your mind and say the word TRUST.

Now put the paper away for a moment and now close your eyes and ask your brain to bring you the image of the word TRUST and also ask your brain to give you a little smile to go with this image of the word TRUST.

Now say to your brain "I trust life and I trust my brain if ever I have a moment of doubt please give me this image of the word TRUST and also give me a smile to reinforce this image"

You may only need to do this once or perhaps a few times. Now we all have doubts and doubtful images flash through our mind I don't think these things can be stopped. But I do know from my own experience if you ask your brain next time a negative image appears in my head or a negative thought enters my head. I want you to instantly replace it with the image of TRUST and then give me a smile to enforce my trust.

When you first begin to get results with this exercise it could be early or it could take some time with me it was early. At the point of your positive results thank your brain and then realise that your best defence against negativity which leads to panic attacks is in your own head.

Now I had some very powerful tools when I needed them; they were smiling and imagery. And when I discovered the importance of the past in my adult behaviour, well, I went back in my mental imagery and I rewrote my anxious childhood experiences.

Rewriting the Past

Many people will tell you to forget about the past. The only problem is they don't tell you how to do it. I have found in my experience that you cannot forget the past, but I have been able to rewrite it in my memory and accept it. Although I had many fearful occasions in my youth, I consider my youth only a bit scarier than the average kid. And there are people who had great struggles in their youth; fortunately for me, I am not one of them.

So rewriting my past and then accepting it was something that I did do successfully. In using imagery to rewrite my past, I did not set lofty goals or seek revenge as I sometimes imagined in my adult life. I went back to times of being over-disciplined or being picked on and embarrassed in front of my friends, and I simply rewrote them with a smile.

I pictured myself after those incidences as standing there and smiling and not being fused. I did not picture the incidences themselves, but when my mind was triggered back to my past by seeing or hearing of something similar when that image appeared, I instantly saw myself smiling. I did this by picturing a mental image of me smiling and at the same time asking my brain to bring me this image when my regretful memory was triggered. And I also asked my brain to give me a genuine smile of accomplishment when this happened. I use the image of TRUST as my first defence against any negative images or thoughts. So now even if my memories go back to an event which caused me resentment, I can genuinely smile.

So rewriting the past has served me well, and it was a genuine tool in recovery from panic attacks.

Listen to Your Body: What Is It Trying to Tell You?

Whether you are experiencing anxiety or an ache, pain, or even an illness, your body is trying to tell you something. And if you look at it as an early warning sign, then perhaps it can be nipped in the bud before things get worse. I read a good piece of information from Louise L. Hay in her book *You Can Heal Your Life*. It goes something like this: "Illness and pain in your body are trying to tell you something." A very simple example may be you have a headache. There could be many reasons why, but your body is trying to tell you to drink water. And since reading that information, I have questioned every ache and pain or anxiety that has come my way. And I usually find that all my aches and pains have something to do with what is happening to me and what is happening in my life. For example, each time I have had a backache, there has been stress in my family life, which I cannot avoid. I can dismiss my own dramas, but other people's dramas do take a small toll on me, even if I say, "It's OK. I can handle this." Other aches and pains in my body have been a sign that I have been pushing myself a bit too hard. And when these signs appear, I quickly slow things down and take things a bit easier. Then there were my nightmare dreams I believe it was my bodies way of telling me to avoid violence. And the biggest examples were the panic attacks. I believe it was my body saying, "Change your negative ways."

So next time you have an illness, an ache, or a pain, by all means take your medication. And perhaps also see if there is a message from your body. Maybe even see what Louise L. Hay recommends in her book. I think you may be surprised.

Expectations:
Just Ease Up on Them

A common theme that I read was having expectations that were too high, which led to disappointment, and disappointment leads to negative emotions. It was only natural for me to want everything to be good because that is human nature. In life, I always tried my best, but I found out that the results that came my way varied regardless of how much effort I put in and how much I wanted them to be good. Not only me. I have seen the best athletes in the world perform well below expectation. Expectation anxiety will hinder performance at times. From my own experience having high expectations and not meeting them starts that argument in your head which causes problems.

Now my expectations are loving life, which brings me peace. Loving life is a choice. I have placed no demands on life. My love for life is unconditional. I have not said that when I have the best of this and when my wealth equals this and when these expectations are met that I will love life.

Life is what it is and I cannot change it. They say, "You get out of life what you put into it." How true. I put love into my life and I get love back in return. I don't have lofty expectations. I have learnt to accept whatever life gives me, and everyday life is beautiful no matter what it is.

Learn to Accept or Like What You Are Doing

Learn to accept or like what you are doing. It sounds hard, but it is achievable, and after a while, it becomes easy. I found that I just had to get my brain involved, and then learning to like what I was doing became a game to me. I loved it.

I will give some examples of everyday people including myself who didn't like what they were doing. "I hate my Job" is the most common example. Others are these: "I don't like this." "I can't stand those." "This really irritates me." "That person gets up my nose." "Life sucks." this list could go on, but the longer the list goes on means the more things upset you. Which means if something upsets you, then it really does upset you where you least expect it, and that is in your subconscious mind and in your brain that tug of war.

Now remember your brain will give you whatever it is capable of doing and it can quite easily make you hate something that you should not hate, and the brain can easily irritate you with a rash or something similar. You only have to watch someone who is ranting and raving and watch how their neck goes all red, then they loosen their collar and veins in their neck and forehead swell, and at the same time they are saying, "I can't stand this." At the same time, their brain is saying, "So you can't stand this? OK then, I will make it so uncomfortable for you that you will not be able to stand it". Their brain is now in the negative network producing those chemicals that irritate and give rashes, but only because you asked for it. If you stop and relax and switch to your positive network, things will return to normality. Just allow ninety seconds for those unpleasant chemicals to flush out of the system.

So I hope my message of stop hating or at least learn to accept—or even better, learn to like what you are doing—is conveyed in this last example.

And a common theme with panic-attack sufferers is they have become negatively programmed in their brain and their negative language gives them unpleasant emotions. Then once the emotions arrive, they feel unpleasant and the negative language goes from "I can't stand this" to "I feel dreadful." Then they recognise they don't feel good. Add some catastrophic thinking to it, and there is severe anxiety, and possibly a panic attack. If your negative habit contains the saying, "This is killing me," then I suggest dropping that saying immediately. In our other example, the chemicals for the rash to the neck were instant; killing you will take longer, so don't say it and stop hating things. The more things you dislike or hate the bigger the war in your head and you won't even know that it is happening.

So how do you learn to accept or like what you are doing? Firstly, you must stop using negative language, and this is not that hard to do. Just close your eyes and say to your brain, "Next time I go negative on something, I want you to stop me." You may have to do this a few times, but it will eventually work. What will happen is you will start one of your negative raves and at some point you will catch yourself and your mental argument will stop. At that point, immediately stop raving and say, "Thank you," to your brain. And in my case, add a smile. This lets your brain know it has done a good job or maybe use your TRUST image. This is important, and I persisted with it. Eventually I broke my habit of being negative.

So far, you haven't learnt to accept or like things, but you have at least stopped that habit of being negative. Once the negative habit is broken, then ask your brain to help you see the good in things that once irritated you. It will go something like this: "Please, brain, help me to see good in the things in life that once irritated me. If I can't see the good things, then please help me accept them the way they are. This is the path that I now want to follow in my life." This will get your subconscious and conscious mind snowballing together instead of arguing.

I can hear some people saying, "I want to get rid of panic attacks and not learn to accept or like the things that irritate me." I can see your point. But panic attacks start around that seed of fear and those unpleasant emotions. And that war in your head which you didn't know about.

So learning to accept or like the everyday things that irritate us is very important. I am talking here about the necessities of life things like work, play, neighbours, people, cultures, sport, foods, transport, etc. I'm not asking you to like dreadful things like murder or natural disasters. If you absolutely cannot bring yourself to like the everyday things that you once disliked, then at least try to accept them to the point where they stop giving you negative mental emotions.

Until now, you probably did not associate disliking things with panic attacks, but it is all part of a very big picture. If you constantly dislike things and you are always telling yourself that, then your brain will set you up into opposition to all the things you dislike. And some of those things in life are a necessity and cannot be avoided. And the more you dislike them, even hating them, the more your brain will fight against them and you will have a mental war raging in your head next time you are confronted with one of your dislikes. In the end, you are only fighting yourself and you can never win a fight against yourself. Because the harder you fight yourself, the more pain you will inflict on yourself, and it will get worse. You could punish yourself into a panic attack. So don't punish yourself with disliking things. Firstly, learn to stop talking negatively about them, and then try to accept them. At best, learn to like or appreciate them.

At first, I learnt to stop being critical, then I was able to accept things, then I was able to appreciate things, then my eyes were able to see the good in everything and there were no more wars in my head. Life became beautiful, and I am so much better off for it.

Now Learn to Love What You Are Doing

This next subject is my recommendation to people who want to do well in a chosen field, whether that field is work, sports, academics, music, or whatever. I was taught in New Age thinking to be really good at something. You have to love what you are doing. When I discovered how my brain works to retain memory and to pass exams, I loved learning. Hence, I became very good at learning this was my personal experience.

The most common way of achieving is to set a goal and then build your skill level to achieve it. Personally, I don't believe saying you want to be number one in the world will help you achieve your best or saying that winning is all that counts. These may be seen as noble thoughts, and some people will say this kid has the right attitude, but only one kid makes it to number one in the world, and not all kids can win. There is a saying it is "the weight of expectation," and the higher that expectation, then the heavier the weight, which can stifle performance. And I believe the reason is when expectations are not met the war in the head begins. The war is between the high expectations and the low results and as the war continues the gap between expectations and the results increases. I only know this from personal experience.

I believe putting love of your chosen field before results and lofty expectations is the best way of achieving your highest potential this ends the mental war it unites your brain and begins the positive snowball. You can ask your brain to help you to love your chosen field and to open your eyes in finding ways to continually love what you are doing. And as you keep loving what you are doing, your ability will keep growing in it. It is worth trying; it won't cost you anything.

If a young child or even an adult was to ask me how he can achieve the best that he possibly can in his chosen field, I would say, "Learn to love it." I would say, "Ask life to open your eyes to continually find ways to love your chosen field. And when you do love it, ask for even more ways to love it, and you do this by using your brain correctly. Don't let results get in the way of your love for your chosen field. The results will come later from your passion to keep growing and loving what you are doing.

It will be easy to know if you are heading in the right direction because you will be enthusiastic about work and looking forward to it. When you turn up, you will be smiling and looking to improve your skill and your ability. Your employer will be glad he or she hired you and *All* because you love your work. Or your coach will be impressed with your ability. Remuneration is important, but if you love what you are doing, remuneration is not everything.

If by some chance you lose your love for what you are doing, do not be discouraged. See it as a sign that life has sent you to look elsewhere. At least you did not continue in that field to the point where it became a burden to you.

Don't Label Yourself

"Don't label yourself" is a common theme that I read in most self-help books. Sometimes I wonder how everyone else knew except me. If the labels you use are positive, such as, "I'm a person who loves life," then keep using them and keep up the good work. But most labels are negative, such as "I'm hard on myself," "I'm a person who punishes himself to get the best results," "I can't live with myself" "I get so angry with myself" "I believe in no pain, no gain," "I hate this," "That makes me sick," or "This is killing me." Or labels to illnesses, like "I'm an allergy sufferer," "I' m a panic-attack sufferer," "I'm a migraine sufferer," or "I am always sick."

Let me give you some examples that I commonly once used to describe myself.

Firstly, I hate the cold. Secondly, the cold makes me miserable. Thirdly, I get the flu twice every year. And at the time, I truly believed these statements but I stopped using those labels and in the past two years, I have not had the flu. I have stopped hating the cold, and I am no longer miserable in the wintertime. Three months of every year are winter, so if you say you hate the cold and it makes you miserable, then that is what your brain will have you believe—but only because you keep saying it. I changed my language to this: "Winter is OK." And in the last two years, I have not had the flu. I barely had to take anything for flu symptoms and I am comfortable with winter.

Now I know there are a lot of people with genuine illnesses and genuine pain, so don't give up your medication; continue to see your doctor. But in my case, I gave myself labels to genuine long-term pain that I was suffering.

Now in these next two examples, I was taking long-term medication to genuine pain that I was suffering

The labels I used were that I have a bad back and that I have tennis elbow. Now all my working life, I had a bad back. In my twenties, I narrowly avoided surgery because I chose to put up with the pain. I had tennis elbow for ten years and had many injections in my left elbow, and both my elbows had been bandaged for years.

Now after reading, don't label yourself. I dropped the labels and began specific exercise programs and continued with the medication until the pain went. Then the pain went, and the need for medication went with it. Now that was over two years ago, and this has also helped reduce my anxiety through living a healthy, pain-free life, and all that I did was drop the labels. I was always exercising. I just changed the exercise programs to accommodate the injuries.

So I dropped the labels and my attachment to them, and they rapidly disappeared. The most common label that I now use is this: "I'm someone who loves life." And I labelled *life* "beautiful," and in my internal language, I labelled my brain and myself "beautiful," and most things in life I label as "beautiful." This is just part of my positive snowball. I believe dropping the labels united my brain in my effort to recover.

Doing Something Because It Is the Right Thing to Do

After my experience with panic attacks, I read all the books and took all the professional advice, because I had one objective: to get rid of panic attacks. So I set about following all that good advice to rise above panic attacks. It worked for me, and it will work for you.

I followed all the good advice like forgetting about the past and not worrying about the future. I learnt to forgive and to forget about revenge. I had to learn how to accept and not to hate. I also learnt not to discriminate. Only after making these changes, I truly learnt real acceptance. And I did all this with the intention of rising above panic attacks, and I did rise above them, and I accomplished what I set out to do.

However, looking back now with a clear head and a sound mind, I only did these things to rise above panic attacks. It plainly occurs to me now that this is how I should have led my life anyway. It is now obvious to me that this is what I needed to do to rise above panic attacks: just lead a better life. At the time, I only did it because all the advice pointed to it, and now I realise that this is how I want to lead my life because "it is the right thing to do." Not just because I wanted to solve a problem in my life.

I have done things in my life because they were the right thing to do, but they usually involved helping others. I helped many friends. Some were in difficult times, and I thought nothing of it because it just seemed right to help out. I don't intend to change my helping ways, but this time I am going to including helping myself. Leading my new life with trust in myself and love and respect for myself is something I did not do in the past, but all that has changed now. And it only seems right if I am going to treat myself in this newfound manner that I also treat others the same way, because it is the right thing to do.

What I Believe about Myself

Since the panic days, the biggest thing that changed in my life was the way I looked at life. And many of those changes were beliefs about myself.

Here are some beliefs that I discovered that help me in my direction of peace in my life.

In the book *You Can Heal Your Life* by Louise L. Hay, I read some lines which read, "It is true if you believe it to be true" and "Whatever I choose to believe becomes true for me." These two lines have helped me immensely in my new direction of positivity in my life. Let me explain something about me, which I believe is true to me and which I have worked out for myself. Now the next few lines may not agree totally with modern psychology, but I believe that they are true to me and that is what counts here. They are true to me.

1. I believe that my brain is a highly intelligent thinking machine that has all the knowledge that I need to help me with life. I also believe that my brain operates in the now and responds to all my needs as they arise.

2. I believe that my subconscious is where my old fears and false beliefs about the past and the future lay, and I firmly believe that now that I am addressing these old problems that my subconscious is becoming more positive. Therefore, I am growing in confidence and trust.

3. I believe that my subconscious, which is concerned about the past and future, occupies space in my brain, my brain which is dealing with the now. And although they both live in my head, I believe that they are two different identities.

4. I believe that when I feel anxiety and fear in my body, it is my subconscious mind which is concerned. The best way to address its concerns is for me to take leadership and also ask my brain to help ease the concerns of my subconscious mind.

5. I believe that I ask my in the now brain to help me ease the concerns of my subconscious mind when there is some fear and anxiety. This ends the mental divide between the two and begins

the positive snowball rolling uniting them in the direction of peace in my body.

For example, when I feel anxiety, my self-talk will be this: "My beautiful brain, our little mate is worried. I can feel it. Can you help me to ease his concerns and help him out?" Our little mate is our subconscious mind. I believe that for me this is the correct direction, because it does ease my concerns and my anxiety and I will continue to correct the past mistakes, false beliefs, false labels, and false sayings that my subconscious mind has had to endure. I know this to be true because I have lessened my anxiety by 99 percent, and I know I must continue to work at it for the rest of my life and not let the old bad habits of war creep back into my head.

Now most people talk to themselves and I do too my only difference is I talk to my brain or I talk to my subconscious or I talk to me.

Leadership and the Confident Leader combined with Likeness and the Power of Attraction

There is definitely a power of attraction, and from what I have read in books and from what I have experienced, I know it to be true.

Let's briefly go back to that smile. People who smile attract other people who smile. The opposite is true. Anger attracts anger, and fear attracts fear. If a person is fearful, particularly a leader, then the followers will pick up on that fear and they too will become fearful. And the opposite is true. If a leader is confident and relaxed, then the people they are leading become more confident and more relaxed.

When it comes to panic attacks, you have to be the confident leader and you must trust your positive brain. Together, you will install confidence in your struggling subconscious mind, and you will unite and be one eventually you will prevail so you must also have patience and TRUST.

Later, the section titled "Dealing with a Panic Attack" we will go into detail of how you, the confident leader, and your intelligent brain will guide your fearful subconscious mind through a difficult situation. Until the concerns of your subconscious mind are eased and confidence returns to your body in the form of less anxiety and more peace.

Patience

Patience is something that I have had to learn, particularly in recovering from those panic days. And it has improved greatly, but deep in my subconscious I know I have a long way to go. For example, in the old, negative days, it may have looked as if I was patient on the outside by remaining calm. But inside, I would be building with emotion. Patience and faith in oneself are so important in recovering from panic. Never give yourself a timetable to recover. Just trust, have patience, and have faith that it will happen the more trust the sooner the result.

But I know that deep in my subconscious there is more room for improvement. Because even though I am positive and committed and in a good frame of mind about a project, I can tell that my subconscious is impatient and wants to get the job done with. I am making big progress with my patience. This book has become a project for me now, and I have had to learn patience with writing it. And my patience with it has improved greatly from that time when I had to take a break from it.

Patience was a problem in our family. Everything had to be done *right now* when I was growing up, and I am working on erasing that belief. In my adult life, my belief and attitude was to "get stuck in" and complete things. Many times, the need to finish so quickly caused me many sleepless nights and anxiety. There is a time and place for this attitude of "getting stuck in," but it is not an attitude that I recommend living your life by—but only when it is genuinely needed. It puts unneeded pressure on you and unneeded pressure on your family.

Also in my early years at school, I tested the teacher's patience even as early as the third grade. Teachers thought that I was being a smarty by playing dumb and not answering them. In each occasion, they lost their temper with me. The truth is I just did not know the answers, so as their demands got louder and louder and more furious, I just froze and became tongue-tied. I was unable to answer, which led to forgettable scenes. So I have some patience repairs that need mending in my subconscious, and I think that they are largely completed now.

Be the Person You Want Others to Be

There are many different types of personalities in this world, and most of them are a joy to be with. Some can be very hard to deal with, and they cause you anxiety. We have all heard the saying, "You can't change someone who does not want to change." And from my experience, that is 100 percent true. But you can act like the person you want them to be.

In my old days I confronted angry people with the same amount of anger I was receiving. I no longer do that it was hard at first to not state my opinion and argue with them. Now I just try and act the way I would like them to act and confrontations are avoided. This has also helped reduce my overall anxiety.

CHAPTER 8

What Worked and What Didn't Work for me When Dealing with Panic Attacks

Now when I was living with the panic attacks, I looked for information to help me deal with them. No one that I knew personally had ever spoken about panic attacks, so there was no advice from someone with firsthand experience. I could not buy a book off the shelf that was specific to panic attacks. Most of the books I read were about leading a better life and dealing with health issues and the brain. I did download some information from the Internet, and then there were people who thought they knew how to solve your problem by giving advice. Very few people knew about my panic attacks, and the only small amount of advice that I got did not work, because if the authors hadn't been there, then they couldn't have understood.

My anxiety came in four stages: mild anxiety, medium anxiety, high anxiety, and finally panic attacks. So I will describe each level of anxiety and the technique that I used to deal with each.

1. Mild anxiety: an unsettled stomach and very little appetite.
2. Medium anxiety: feeling ill, light pins and needles in the forearms, and heart racing at about eighty beats per minute.
3. High anxiety: intense pins and needles in the forearms, unable to keep still and feeling ill in the stomach, and feeling the need to throw up, heart racing well above one hundred beats per minute, and feeling an intense rise in body temperature.

4. A panic attack: heart racing so fast it hurt my chest, usually reduced to the floor, perspiring profusely, body shaking and struggling to breath.

So now I will give you a list of things that I tried and how much effect each one had on me. In the first three months, the only thing that stopped a panic attack was Valium tablets. Everything else that I tried failed. After three months, I was having some success. This is the list I tried after that third month, with limited success as my approach began to change to acceptance and no more verbal abuse.

1- Breathing exercises and breathing into a brown paper bag: did not prevent a panic attack, but correct breath*ing* is a must-do to prevent things from getting even worse.
2- Meditation: during high anxiety it did not work. I tried meditation, but I was unable to keep still. These days, I meditate at night to help clear my mind and fall asleep.
3- Music: in high anxiety, I tried soft music and loud music, and they did not prevent a panic attack. Although I now enjoy listening to relaxing music, it still only helps in mild anxiety.
4- Dancing: during high anxiety, I tried dancing, and it did not prevent a panic attack.
5- Walking: slow walking helps during medium anxiety, but if anxiety is already up to high level, not even walking helped.
6- Reading: inspirational verses from a book. Did not work.
7- Relaxing on the lounge: during anxiety did not work. I was unable to keep still.
8- Talking to someone: did not work.
9- Exercise: did not work. Only helped with mild anxiety.
10- Tough love: telling myself to snap out of it. Just do not speak to yourself like that. It only makes things worse.
11- Fighting: I tried bravado by saying to my panic attacks, "You can't hurt me. I'm not scared of you." This only made things worse.
12- Empathy: this worked many times. I said things like, "I understand, mate. It will be OK," and did continuous positive talk. I would begin talking to myself from the early stage of mild

anxiety, and many times it stopped right there. If anxiety hit me at stage-three level, empathy worked. If it improved slightly, slow walking helped, and then positive self-talk and staying in the now. This combination worked.

13- Being in the now: trying to concentrate on a fixed point or staring at the wall and focusing my attention to divert my mind from the anxiety and to bring my attention into the present moment. This did not work on its own I now realise my brain was in the now but my subconscious was elsewhere dealing with fear. But being in the now is very important along with positive encouragement with your brain and subconscious and some slow walking it did work.

There is no one-only thing that will beat panic attacks it takes a positive lifestyle and a combination of many positive things which will need change and a little time.

There are two very important topics to cover before we go on to dealing with panic attacks. They are fighting panic attacks and accepting panic attacks.

Now if I asked most people which is the most positive way to deal with a panic attack—fight them or accept them—the vast majority would say you have to be positive and fight them. And they would be wrong. Most people who fight their panic attacks end up like I did when I was fighting them and losing. Fighting them begins the mental war in your head and you cannot win.

If I said the positive way to beat panic attacks was to accept them, most people would say that is negative because you are giving in. But in life, when not everything makes sense, sometimes you have to do the opposite to what everyone else is telling you. Acceptance begins uniting the brain into one.

So I will have to explain my thinking on this one. Firstly, I will explain why fighting panic attacks is negative.

A common theme I read was to not fight because when you fight you lose they were not talking about panic attacks but fighting in general. And when it comes to fighting panic attacks, losing was exactly what I experienced. When it comes to fighting, you usually have to overcome your opponent with overwhelming force. That makes sense. He uses all the force he has, but you apply greater force and you win. Now when you are having a panic attack, your body uses a huge amount of energy, and that energy is you. So if that panic-attack energy is you and you fight that energy, then you are only fighting yourself. So your opponent, the panic attack, is using almost all of your energy. If you try to fight it and use what is left, soon you will be exhausted and a collapse will not be far away. It is a no-win situation fighting yourself in a panic attack. The more energy you use, the more energy the panic attack uses until there is no energy left.

In martial arts they teach; an opponent who has overwhelming force can be defeated by using his own energy against him. In panic attacks if your own energy is the panic attack then don't fight it, conserve your energy and outlast it and you will avoid it. As in martial arts it will need tactics and your tactics will be acceptance and your positive network which will unite you.

Now accepting your panic attack is the best way to go, and for me it was the only way to go. Your body is much tougher than you think. There were times that, rather than take a tablet, I waited out a panic attack, and I outlasted two panic attacks that lasted seven hours each of continuous high to medium anxiety. Now if I had fought against these panic attacks, I would have lasted only twenty minutes until the point of collapse.

As my acceptance and positive snowball grew, I no longer had to wait so long to ride out a panic attack. For many people try to wait out and accept it, but if you need medication and it is causing you too much stress, then take the medication. There are no losers here. You had a go; that is the main thing. But know that in the future, as your new positive skills and positive life improve, you will rise above panic attacks.

We will soon talk our way through a panic attack. This is a method I would use now. The method that I used during the panic-attack days was mainly positive self-talk with acceptance. But since then, I have discovered the importance of the subconscious mind, and I have improved on that method. Although I have not had a panic attack now for over two years, I have used this method as preventative maintenance every day and also to ride out smaller, less frequent anxiety events.

First Some Revision

Buy now you would have come to terms with the five essential first steps: admit that you have a problem with panic attacks, take responsibility, make peace with your past, stop worrying about the future and have learnt acceptance, and discover the importance of faith in life. And you may have completed the imagery exercise with the word TRUST.

You may have discovered what your greatest fear was and have begun to address it. For me, it was embarrassment and criticism, and I addressed it by going back mentally in my past and rewriting the incidences with positive outcomes. Also, if you have not humbly apologised to your brain if you were a person who regularly called himself names, then apologise to your brain now and unite your brain.

And by now you know that you must take the lead and have faith in your own ability to succeed. It is OK to ask for help spiritually from God, the universe, or life and for help from friends, doctors, psychologists, or medication. But in the end, they cannot solve your problems; they can only help. It is you who must lead and do the hard work and have TRUST.

Now during this panic-attack simulation, there will be three main entities which are involved: you, the confident leader who is feeling the anxiety; your intelligent, helping brain, which has all the equipment to help you through it; and your subconscious mind, which is afraid and anxious. And you are also feeling its pain. And when it is over you will all become one.

At first, I used images of my subconscious as a nervous little child. But now that I have become more confident, when anxiety arrives, I just address my subconscious as my little mate without the need for a mental image. If adding images to your subconscious helps you, then go ahead; an image can be an inspiring tool.

Now during a panic attack, and after recovery from panic attacks, or in your new beautiful life, when positive emotions come your way because of some pleasant experience or a triumph over a difficulty, never use terms like "This is so good, I can't believe this is happening." And don't say, "This is too good to be true" or "this is too good to be happening to me." Although these sayings sound positive and thankful, but your ever obedient brain will put an end to your recovery right there instantly I know, because you unknowingly told it that it can't be true or it is too good for you. Use other positive language.

Remember a well-trained brain has all the answers to solve your problems. So when these positive emotions come your way, just know that you are on the correct path to bigger and better things and let these small rewards of positive emotion be your motivation to persist in your new direction. After all, you are worthy of a beautiful life; you just have to believe it.

Dealing with a Panic Attack

So we will pretend that you have woken up in the morning and you are not feeling well. Later that morning, you must attend an event which is giving you anxiety. At that very first incidence of acknowledging your feelings, you will accept them with positivity and honesty, and it will sound like this:

1. "I'm feeling a bit off or I'm not feeling well right now, but that's OK. I know it will get better." By saying this, you have accepted your anxiety and avoided a fight with yourself that would have quickly drained your energy. Accept your anxiety as someone who needs help. In this case, the anxiety is the fear of your subconscious mind who needs help. And you have now united your brain. I will now refer to my subconscious mind as "my little mate." The next step is to engage your positive thinking brain with honesty. And it will go like this:

2. "My beautiful brain, our little mate is worried and I am feeling his pain. I know you have all the tools to help me ease his concerns. Together we can get him through this." All this is internal language to yourself. There is no need to speak out aloud unless you wish to do so. The next step is for you to talk directly to your subconscious mind and pledge your assistance, and it will sound like this:

3. "Hello, little mate. I know you are struggling because I can feel your pain. I know you are worried, and that is OK. I understand you have memories and instinct from our past, which gives you concern. But times have changed now and we are in control of our own lives. TRUST me, little mate, my brain and I are with you all the time, and we will never let you down."

Now all this internal language would have happened as soon as those unpleasant emotions were felt, perhaps from the moment you woke up or later that morning. Or maybe you had a sleepless night. When doubtful thoughts or images enter your head use your TRUST image in your brain to deal with them. After this third step the three identities are now uniting as one.

4. By now, you are up and about. I found movement helped with my anxiety. If you are off frequently to the bathroom, that is OK. It is your fight or flight system preparing you to work, not preparing you to fight. Your body thinks that this event you are attending later on is very important, and it is sending you to the bathroom regularly as part of your preparation. Do not misinterpret this as being ill. Although you may feel ill, it is nature's way of preparing you. It will get better just TRUST. You will be continuing your positive self-talk with honesty. And even try a small smile as you are going through your positive internal language.

Continue reassuring your subconscious with positivity and understanding. Your brain is using its positive network to help your subconscious, which in turn helps reduce your anxiety. Now do not at any point go negative if relief has not yet arrived. If you stumble and give in to negativity or negative emotions, remember what we quoted earlier. You will have to wait at least ninety seconds for that chemical to flush out of your system. Your brain is also capable of producing calming chemicals, but you will have to stay in the positive circuitry for your brain to produce them.

5. As soon as you feel any relief, like a lessening in anxiety or a feeling of increased confidence, let that little small smile on your face turn into a large smile, and at the same time thank your brain for its assistance. Continue the patient encouragement to your subconscious.

6. Now all your positive self-talk between you and your subconscious will continue to revolve around patience and encouragement TRUST and eventually thanks for your subconscious. The positive self-talk between you and your brain will revolve around thanking your brain for its assistance in helping your little mate and reinforcing the TRUST in your brain and congratulating your brain for a job well done, all along reinforcing this gratitude with a smile. And finally, thank yourself for persevering and give yourself a huge smile to ingrain it in your newly trained subconscious memory. When you achieve your success over the panic register that feeling in your body and in your brain at this point you have become one.

If, however, relief is taking longer than you would like, remember you are much tougher than you think, and by not fighting your anxiety, you can conserve your energy for a long time if that is what you wish to do. But if anxiety is overwhelming you and you have spoken to your doctor about it, then help yourself with medication. But each time you take that medication, just say to yourself with positivity and honesty, "I am thankful for the relief this medication gives me, but I know that one day I will be able to reduce my dependency on it, and I know as my positive network grows one day I will be able to rise above panic attacks on my own."

So that is how I do it. I have not had to fend off a panic attack for over two years now. But I use this exact positive technique to deal with any anxiety which arises. I also use the same positive technique when I am feeling well every day as my preventative maintenance. By reassuring my subconscious mind with positive thoughts and by using my brain correctly and having TRUST to create that positive superhighway and build my positive snowball.

The Magic Pill

During those panic days, I tried many cures and remedies that were suggested to me by professional people or that I read about in books or over the Internet. Some helped ease my anxiety, and some didn't. I found that a commitment to a positive lifestyle and a positive re-education of my brain is what dissolved my panic attacks.

When I first had the panic attacks, I was looking for a magic pill to cure my problem. In my case, Valium calmed me enough to help me deal with the next panic attack, but it was no magic pill. It was the first time in my life that I needed to take them. But Valium does not prevent the reason why the panic attacks happen. I dreaded the thought of another episode of panic that I would have swallowed any legal drug. When there was no magic pill, I looked for the next best thing. I thought there must be some book or text somewhere that would act like a magic pill.

I was looking for a quick fix. I put my life on hold for a few weeks, but my life had to go on. But like I said, there is no instant cure of panic attacks that any one trip to a specialist or one tablet will prevent. It takes a commitment to change a lifestyle. The commitment to the change can be done instantly, but the change itself will take time. It can take a long time depending on how closely you are attached to your old lifestyle. But if you are committed and change your ways, I believe early results will come in just a few months and your early results will drive your desire to change. This is where patience is required. But it will be your incoming positive results that will be your guidance and proof to a life of peace then joy.

Correct Positive Thinking versus Negative Thinking

The importance of thinking cannot be understated. To sum it up, if you think sad, dreadful, and fearful thoughts for long enough, then eventually you will feel sad, dreadful, and fearful. And if you think positive and peaceful thoughts for long enough, then eventually you will begin to feel positive and peaceful. Thinking one positive thought when you are about to have a panic attack is not going to instantly dissolve your fear and avert a panic attack, but it is a start. Living a life of positive thoughts is what will keep panic attacks away by dealing with them at the anxiety level. By reducing your anxiety, ridding out your anxiety, or at least managing your anxiety to a level which allows you to continue on with your life.

Thinking is something that my mind does continually, even when I am not aware of it, and there are times when I can actually switch my mind off from thinking. But sooner rather than later, my mind will sneak in and start thinking again. And I have learnt that my mind is incredibly persistent, so why not just go with it rather than fight it? I read once whenever you fight you lose, so if my mind continually wants to think, then it is up to me to train my brain to think correctly. After all, I want to be in control of my mind, because with panic-attack sufferers, it is their mind which is in control of them.

To me, there are three types of thinking. There is negative thinking, which there is no place for. There is positive thinking with unrealistic expectations, which I still do not recommend. And there is positive thinking with honesty, which I do recommend. It is hard to define negative and positive thinking. I looked around and found some long-winded answers and other sources had no answers, so I will use some examples to get my message across. So let's get negative thinking out of the way first.

Negative Thinking

The first and only rule with negative thinking is that it has no place in your brain. It is OK to sensibly look at things and see the pitfalls and address them. Like that job I am applying for. Do I have the skills and the ability to deal with it? It is OK to ask these questions of yourself. This is not negative thinking; it is human nature. But if you answer yourself with, "No way. You are stupid, remember?" then that is negative thinking and it has no place in your brain.

Another example of negative thinking is reverse psychology like trying to motivate yourself by calling yourself stupid and telling yourself that you will never be any good in the hope that it will have the reverse effect and you will get the job done. And I say, "Don't do it." I used this method all my life, and it greatly contributed to my panic attacks. And don't tell yourself or people they are not capable of doing something, even if your intentions are good and you want to see them succeed, because for the rest of their lives they will remember your disbelief in them.

And then there is just plain old negative thinking: "The world sucks then you die." "I hate this and I hate that." "This makes me sick." Just do not say these things because remember what I said earlier: your brain is an incredible thing, and if it is capable of doing something, it will. So if you say things like "This makes me sick" or "I can't take it anymore," your brain is quite capable of delivering these thoughts to you subconsciously. You will be sick and you will not be able to take it anymore. Just do not use negative thinking. There is no place for it at all. It is OK to question things constructively and see the pitfalls;

So I have now established there is no place for negativity in my life, and that is that.

Positive Thinking with Unrealistic Expectations

Not all positive thinking is good. Some positive thinking is unrealistic and sets you up for anxiety when results do not come your way. With children, there are three common things which most are exposed to: education, sports, and then work as they get older. To tell a child that he can become number one in his school, to tell a child that he can become number one in his chosen sport, to tell a young adult that he can become the best in his chosen field, or to tell a child that winning is the only thing that matters—all these things sound like positive thinking, and it depends on how you look at them. If you set your ambitions too high before you begin and then the results are not coming your way then anxiety will set in caused be the divide between expectation and results the greater the divide then the greater the war in your head. And the higher the target like being number one, the higher the weight of expectation. keep your goals realistic and learn to enjoy what you are doing and let results happen do not force them.

There was a time when my own positive goals were too high and the anger and frustration it caused me when I did not meet my own high expectations. So that is why positive thinking with honesty is in my experience the correct positive thinking.

Positive Thinking with Honesty

I have so many experiences with positive thinking with honesty over the last three years that I would like to share them with you and how they helped me rise above panic attacks and greatly reduce my anxiety. Going back to those days of panic, I could not see anything good in my life. I was a negative thinker when it came to my own situation. But all the books said to use positive language and positive thinking, and I did, but I wanted instant results. Although the results started to happen after six months or so, I believe that if I had approached them with realistic honesty, I could have achieved those results sooner.

For example, when I was at my worst, I commenced my positive thinking by saying affirmations things like, "I'm going to fight this; I won't be beaten by panic attacks," "I feel great I can do anything I like," and "I'm not afraid of panic attacks." These sound like positive thoughts, but at the time, they simply were not true to me. At the time, I was fighting panic attacks and they were beating me. I didn't feel great. I felt awful, and I was afraid of panic attacks. If I was to say those things now, they would be true. I am not afraid of panic attacks and I do feel great, but that is now.

Then I read about acceptance and honesty with oneself, so then my positive self-talk and affirmations sounded like "I am struggling at this stage of my life and it is difficult for me, but I know that someday it will turn around for the better" and "I accept panic attacks as something that has happened to me, and I am afraid of them now but I have faith in the universe and I know that if I persevere things will get better." Also, "Thank you for this stage in my life. I know all the difficult times I have experienced in the past have led to better things, and I have faith that someday I will be in a better place than I am now." When I accepted my situation with honesty and stopped fighting it I ended the war in my head and united my brain as ONE.

Now I know that the first three affirmations about fighting panic attacks and feeling great and not being afraid sound positive, and they were, but they had only a minimal effect on my improvement, although they were much better than any negative talk. The other three affirmations were honest and they had a huge effect on me. After saying affirmations with honesty according to my situation, my brain seemed to snap into gear and unite, particularly the bit about faith and believing and TRUST that things will someday be better.

Looking back, I realise why my affirmations had to be honest to my situation for two reasons. Even my brain knows when I am not telling the truth. Your brain is very intelligent and it can be guided in the right direction but you have to unite it and you have to be honest with it to guide it correctly. The other reason is your negative network is so large and powerful that you must slowly work your way into it with honesty like getting your foot in the door and gradually opening it. Trying to trick your negative network by telling it you are not afraid doesn't work it keeps the war going on, your brain is too intelligent for that. Instead you must start at the foundation of your negative network and then gradually over power it with your positive network.

Apart from the early months after I accepted panic attacks, I put myself under no pressure to improve by having faith in the universe, and saying that someday it will get better. It felt like a burden of expectation had been lifted from my shoulders.

Before that, my positive talk revolved around fighting back and deadlines and not being beaten, and although my motivation was noble, it didn't work. There is no substitute for honesty in any walk of life, and that goes for positive thinking too. No matter how good the intentions are, they still have to be honest and achievable.

Achievable leads me to the next positive affirmations. I didn't ask for anything that I could not achieve myself. At no time did I ask to be number one at anything in the world or did I ask for a magic act to cure me. As I started to see results with my positive self-talk, I only asked for things that I thought the universe and my brain could achieve: "Please help me to be a better person." "Please help me to see things more positively." "Please show me how to lead a better life." "Please point me in the direction of peace." Now I asked the universe to help me with all these requests, but I do know how my brain works and I knew that they were all achievable by my united brain. It is just that I asked the universe to help then my brain pointed these things out to me, and eventually they did come to me. And my recovery was accelerated greatly.

I now believe that when I talk to the universe, or life, my brain is involved, and because I only asked for things that were achievable by me like being a better person, being more positive, leading a better life, and finding peace, I received them. So I can't tell you which one of these things gave me what I asked for, but I have faith in all of them. Faith is everything. Faith in all these things gave me faith in myself and in my beautiful life. So when I thank the universe or life, I also thank my beautiful brain.

So that I do not confuse people with faith when they are looking for guidance, let me explain my theory on my own faith then you can make up your own mind.

I am a very practical person, and once I am shown evidence that something works or exists then I will believe it. So I have faith in the universe, my brain, life, and God. Now I will explain each one.

Firstly, the universe. This is plain and simple. The universe contains everything and it is beautiful, so it is a good place to place my trust. The universe life and love do not discriminate they do not say if you follow these rules you will receive favour, their beauty is available to everyone. I came from the earth, which is part of the universe, and eventually I will go back to the earth. So whether I am here alive or long gone, I will always be part of the universe, and I love it and I am at peace with it.

Then I have faith in my brain, and I totally believe in my brain after being shown how to use it correctly to pass exams and so on. I used the same technique to build my positive snowball, which has made my life so good. The evidence is the turnaround in my life. Then after making important discoveries about my brain, and training my brain correctly my life and attitude improved immensely.

Then there is faith in life. Life is everything, and now I am able to see how beautiful life is. I love my life. I totally believe you can steer your life into a direction, and my direction is peace, which brings me joy. I believe life is what you make it and now I make my life love and peace and my reward is joy.

Now before my panic attacks, I had not even heard of faith in the universe. I was wary of life, and my brain was something that I abused every time I made a mistake.

Fear played the major role in my education it was very scary at times. Some teachers commanded fear and that is how they taught their classes. Not only my education but my faith was reinforced with fear I was taught the fear of God.

Fear should never be used as a learning tool, especially with young children with their vulnerable minds. Fear in education only causes problems, firstly by blocking information from going into your brain and secondly by leaving mental scares on your young subconscious minds. Love solves problems. So along with all the other fears that I had to dispel, I also had to dispel my fear of God.

There you have it: my belief on my faith, how my faith helps me, and what you believe in becomes true to you. That's how your brain works. The more you believe in something, the more real it becomes. So if you believe in a particular religion and you have faith in it, then you can start from there. I love my universe, I love my life, I love my brain, and my loving God, whatever God may be. And love does solve everything and it is available to everyone.

So when I explained my correct positive thinking, I could not explain it without explaining my faith. And to remain positive, I had to change my fear of God to a love of God.

In summing up correct positive thinking, there is a beautiful world out there and it is available to everyone and asking to see the beauty in it would be a good first request. Then like me, most of the other things I wanted I already had. I just couldn't see them.

Catastrophic Thinking

I soon learnt that catastrophic thinking is common to panic-attack sufferers. Catastrophic thinking is the ultimate form of negative thinking. Like the word says, it leads to catastrophe, which combined with the seed of fear that has been growing in them for years builds up into panic attacks. I used to think I was a positive person in life who looked on the bright side of things, but clearly I wasn't. I used to say to people things like, "That's OK, it will be all right" and "Never mind. It's not the end of the world." But that's what I used to say to other people. What I used to say to myself was, "You idiot, you have ruined it." "Don't make a fool of yourself." So you see, I had two standards: one for everyone else, which was a positive standard, and a very tough negative standard for myself.

Now all my life, when preparing for anything, whether it was work, sports, or holidays, I would look at all the things that could go wrong, then I would address them before the event. That way, when that day arrived, I would have all the bases covered. This may sound like a good practice, but I took it too far. When I say I looked at what could go wrong, I would look at it as a catastrophe. So before the event, as I pictured in my mind all the things that could go wrong, little did I know that my brain was recording the catastrophe and then giving me an emotion to go with it, which was anxiety. The emotion would be usually a nervous stomach and an accelerated heart rate, and all I was doing was thinking of the worst thing that could go wrong.

Days later, when the event arrived, I would turn up with my nervous stomach and my accelerated heart rate. Then things would go smoothly, and they usually always went along without a problem. Then when things were nearly over and I could see positive progress, I would eventually calm down, get the job done, and walk away, usually feeling worn out.

Almost every time, things worked out and positive results were achieved, but for days before the event I would continually play over in my mind all the things that could go wrong. At the time, I didn't know what damage I was doing to my subconscious mind I thought that I was doing good preparation. You see, your subconscious mind sees the picture you are developing before the event and records it as an actual event. This is easily proved by thinking of something bad then getting that chill run up your spine or a bad gut feeling the negative damage has been done and all you did was think about it. Consequently, I would turn up to anything feeling very nervous with my pre-recorded negative emotion, and that was before the panic attacks. After the panic attacks, I could not even go shopping, catch a bus, or turn up to any social gathering because my catastrophic thinking had pictured me lying on the ground after having passed out from panic and anxiety. And it had not even happened.

So catastrophic thinking is something you must stop doing. It is OK to think of an upcoming event and do some preparation, but think of it for only a short time and think of the good things which will more than likely happen. I personally deal with upcoming events with an attitude of "It will be whatever it will be." My brain was so trained at looking at the worst things that could possibly happen that I would get many negative visions in my mind. But I have reprogrammed my brain because I have learnt how to use it correctly. I have said to my brain, when I drift off to the future, "I want you automatically to stop me, and at that point say, 'It will be,' and also give me a smile." I don't say it will be OK, because in my experience it has always been OK. And I read to just let things be as they are going to be. It is all about acceptance. For example, before holidays, I would picture the worst things that could go wrong while saying, "I hope this is going to be a good holiday." My mind must have been so confused and I unknowingly commenced another war in my head. But now my brain knows the holiday will be whatever it will be, and I am comfortable with that. So if you would like to stop your mind from wondering off too much into you future ask your brain to catch you when it happens. Perhaps use your TRUST image or ask your brain to give you a message of "it will be" and use a smile each time your brain helps you.

Things I Discovered about Myself Which Have Helped My New Life

Answers to life have kept coming my way and my life destination is peace in my body, and that is less anxiety. After making big improvement in reducing my anxiety, I began realising a lot of my anxiety came from old habits. All my life, I wanted to be smart, and I became very smart, but in my case, being very smart came with compulsive thinking. Once I was shown how to use my brain for education, I would want to be so intelligent on a subject I would begin compulsively thinking about it and looking back it became a habit. I was always doing mathematical equations in my head. When I went back to technical college, it became a game to me. That's how easy it was to get good marks. But good results for me came with constantly thinking about the particular subject. When I made that important discovery, that compulsive thinking woke me up in the middle of the night with the answer to a complex mathematical equation in my head. I discovered being really smart and knowing all the answers to something is not worth my mental peace with all the negative bad habits that I have broken. I also broke the need to be the smartest. After all, I know that if I put my mind to something, I can be very intelligent at it. So now I am putting my mind to discovering peace in my body and my brain is doing a very good job. My brain does this automatically but not compulsively.

One important habit I broke was a lifetime habit of waking up four times per night and going to the bathroom. I am putting this in this book for a few reasons. The first is sleeping eight to nine hours every night without the need to get up improves your well-being, and another reason is I know the older people get, the less sleep they usually get. I know many elderly people who are up many times per night and would love to sleep through the night.

Getting a Good Night Sleep

I discovered all this information on my own after asking myself why I can't get a good night of sleep. The answers came my way, and there were three reasons: anxiety, habits, and nightmares. I used to be a nervous little kid, and when you're nervous, there are many trips to the bathroom even at night. I also used to have nightmare dreams when I was a kid, and I can even remember some of them. The nightmare dreams continued right up to two years ago. So anxiety and nightmare dreams plus the habit of waking up deprived me of a lot of sleep, and now I am catching up on all those lost hours of sleep.

One year after that first panic attack, I found total peace in my body through my waking hours. But at night, I was still waking up from bad dreams. This led me to believe correctly that my in-the-now brain was content but my subconscious mind was uneasy I don't think that example can be argued with not in my case anyway. After following good advice, I stopped watching the daily and nightly news because 99 percent of the news is bad and made up accidents, tragedies, violence, arguments, and gossip. So up till now, I have not watched any news on television or even listened to it on radio for three years, and my mental state is better for it. I no longer have the need to know what is happening.

But my bad dreams had not totally left me, so I made a commitment to stop watching violence on television. Now this is not easy to do because most television after 7 p.m. is violent, and almost all movies contain violence. I also stopped watching reality television shows because I did not like watching contestants who try their best being put down. So after I committed to not watching the news and no violence and no reality television, the bad dreams stopped.

Now I had peace in my waking hours and peace in my sleeping hours and no anxiety, but I still woke up in the night needing to go to the bathroom. Now that I had trained my brain and eased my subconscious mind. It was my bladder that needed to be trained to hold on for eight hours. And this only took a week. At first, I would wake up and I just had to go, but every time I resisted going until it was necessary. Then my trips to the bathroom decreased from four to two then to one until I just fell back to sleep without the need to go. Then one week later I had my first continuous eight-hour sleep in a lifetime and almost every night since with very few exceptions. I do still wake up in my dream state, but because the dreams are not scary or violent, I just roll over and fall asleep again.

So there you have it, those three commitments to stop watching the news and to stop watching violence, which eased my subconscious mind. And training my bladder to hold on has also contributed to my newfound peace. I'm sorry that I had to tell you about going to the bathroom all the time, but anxiety and trips to the bathroom go hand in hand. It was much easier to train my bladder than to stop watching the news. It takes some time for the need to know what is happening to leave you. But once you have lost that need to know, you are pretty close to finding peace and acceptance in your life.

Compulsive Thinking

Let me explain my theory about myself and how eliminating compulsive thinking improved my life. I never considered myself a compulsive thinker. I thought that was a title used to describe other people. But I discovered I was a compulsive thinker, and I also think that a lot of other people are also compulsive thinkers, it is just that they do not realise it.

Life demands that we think, and thinking is unavoidable. You must think your way through life, and that is normal. So in your daily life, as situations arise, you are dealing with them and you are thinking usually without realising it. My problem was when I had idle time, my mind went back to the past or off to the future, and that is what a lot of people do. But my mind went back to the problems of the past and then projected them into my future so those mistakes might not happen again.

I was told by my hypnotherapist/psychotherapist that I was a perfectionist, and until then I did not realise it. My perfection attitude also kept me trapped in compulsive thinking. Whatever I was involved in, I usually got consumed by it to try to be the best at it. Whether it was sports, academics, or building my own furniture, it would have my constant thought. I also realised I got consumed by watching television. It did not matter what I was watching; I got involved mentally and became part of the program. So my sports, work, studies, and television had me consumed, and this got my brain active 100 percent of the time. I found out that it leads to a subconscious mind that is involved 100 percent of the time and very little mental peace.

Now that I know my brain and my mind are involved 100 percent of the time, and I have learnt to just steer them in my new direction and that direction is peace in my body. I have stopped my compulsive thinking, and now I think about my positive snowball and my peace but not compulsively. To people—most people and particularly those who do not know me—I probably seem like some guy who is a bit vague and smiles a lot. And I prefer to be a bit vague rather than to have my mind consumed with information. Because I know when it is time to pay attention, I will.

Compulsive Thinking versus Spontaneity

I am living proof of compulsive thinking versus spontaneity. Now looking back on my life, I can see how much anxiety I gave myself through compulsive preparation and compulsive thinking. I will give an example of me to help get my message across.

Most of my life, I worked for a boss. The supervisor would tell me what was needed, and then I would do my best to not have to bother them until I had accomplished the job. When I was working for a boss, I rarely took any work home with me mentally.

Then promotions came my way, and I became the supervisor. I now had many people working for me. When I went home at night I also took the job home with me, which is part of accepting more authority. But I went too far. It is OK to think about work when you are at home; most people do. But I thought about everyone's problems and tried to solve them mentally, and my mind was continually thinking. I was very good at my job, but it came at the expense of my mental peace.

I know now that I would have done an equally good job if I had left my mental work on the job. By doing this, the next day I would have arrived on the job mentally fresh and alert after a good night sleep and let my spontaneous response take over. The job would have been done to an equal standard, and I would have been spared the compulsive thinking.

In life, you have a position because of the knowledge and experience that you have already gained. Now I know the easiest way to achieve results is to let your TRUST in your spontaneous response take over and spare yourself the compulsive thinking and lack of sleep.

So by adopting this new positive attitude of spontaneity compared to compulsive thinking, it has helped reduce my anxiety greatly. It takes trust in me, my brain, and life, and when it comes to recovery from panic, trust and faith in you and in your life is everything.

Diversions and Anxiety

Diversions is a term used for activities which are used to help divert your mind away from your problems and anxiety. Everyday things like walking, exercise, swimming, music, reading, movies, dancing, meditation, cooking, housework, talking, working, golf, holidays, boating, and driving are normal parts of life. But if they are used to overcome a problem like anxiety or panic, then during this time they are described as a diversion because they divert your attention away from your problem. And when there are no problems and you just like doing them for fun. They are described as hobbies, fun, sports, or life.

So there were times when I used a diversion and it worked, and I incorrectly thought that I found a cure for my anxiety. Then the next time anxiety came my way, I would use my newfound cure and it didn't work. So I would try *another* diversion. I found the best diversion for me was walking slowly, but you can't walk forever so the problem still has to be addressed.

My personal experience with diversions—the word *diversions* says it all. I found in my experience that they do help divert my attention in cases of mild anxiety. But I have to admit without the field of psychology pointing me in the correct direction I would be stuck in a world of anxiety. My brain could not help me if I did not know or believe in something.

Before the panic attacks, I thought psychology and looking into your past were excuses for things that went wrong in your life, and I was wrong. Now I believe in the correct use of psychology, and that belief helped engage my brain. For anything to work effectively, you must believe in it, and my brain believes in psychology. I only had two trips to a psychologist because my life was too busy at the time, but work helped slightly as a diversion. Then I had three trips to a hypnotherapist who was also a psychotherapist, and many of the books that I read revolve in some way around psychology. So then I was pointed in the direction of psychology, and the rest of the answers came from asking myself and my brain. I have heard of people and I have met a person who had electric shock treatment and this I would never agree with in all cases these people were unable to overcome their problems.

So I did like my diversions, and they helped me with my mild anxiety at the time. And when there is no anxiety, they are no longer diversions; they are a sport, a hobby, or a joy. But now, as my anxiety has lessened greatly and continues to decline, these things are no longer diversions for anxiety. They bring me even more joy in my new peaceful life.

The Correct Way to Ask the Universe and Your Brain

Now in my recovery from panic attacks, the first book that I read was Louise L. Hay's *You Can Heal Your Life*. She speaks of the beauty and the power of the universe and attracting things, and I agreed with most of what she said; it made sense to me. So when I looked for strength and guidance back then, I asked the universe to guide me. And I still do ask the universe, but now that I have learnt to love life and myself and my brain as much as I love the universe, things have changed slightly. I will ask the universe or I will ask life or I will ask my brain, and I give them all the same amount of importance and love. But asking the universe is where it all began, and then I discovered the importance of my brain in my recovery, so when I asked the universe I also included my brain.

When asking for anything, there is a correct way and an incorrect way. Firstly, the incorrect way to ask for anything is to demand it, and secondly, the correct way of asking is to say, "Please." If you demand something from someone, you are more than likely not going to get it. If you ask someone and then say please, then your chances of receiving are increased. Then if you add a reason why you need it and use humility, your chances of receiving it are greatly increased. And if what you are asking of someone costs that person nothing and you have used humility and you have given a reason why you need it, and you have said please, what reasonable person could say no? That's how I see the universe—something that is totally reasonable. And because I believe in the power and beauty of the universe, I figured if I'm asking, this would be my best chance at getting it.

My first request to the universe was this: "Please, universe, give me the strength and the guidance to beat these panic attacks. I am not asking you to do it for me. Please show me the direction so I can help myself." And things slowly did get better; I did not ask for a miracle or to end my panic attacks immediately. I only asked for strength and guidance. As things were getting better and my life had to go on, I had put my trust in the universe, so I made a second request.

My second request to the universe was this: "Please, universe, can you open my eyes so I can learn to find peace and learn to love life?" And my life continued to get better, then I started discovering how important it was to change my negative ways, and I learnt the importance of using my brain correctly. I discovered that demanding anything divides your brain, and asking with humility and love and saying please unites your brain. Discoveries and improvements began to happen, and they snowballed to where I am today.

I believe that asking for ways to love life was a shortcut to asking for everything in life, because since I made that request, I have everything I need for a loving, peaceful life. I always had everything I needed for a loving, peaceful life. I just couldn't see it. Remember that I asked, "Please open my eyes," and the universe sure did that.

I still ask the universe, but now that I know how important my brain is I ask my brain things too. I believe my brain is like one of those faithful puppy dogs who loves his master and when given a scent runs off all happy and excited to find it and please his master. I don't take that love for granted either. I love my brain, and in return, when I get the answer to a previously asked question to my brain, I smile and say, "Thank you," to my brain and tell my brain how intelligent it is. That may sound nutty to some people, but it works for me and I love it.

In my case, I wanted to get over panic attacks so I asked the universe and I did get over the panic attacks.

CHAPTER 9

Peace and Joy

Don't Look for Happiness; Look for Peace

This is another beautiful piece of information I read from Eckhart Tolle's book *The Power of Now*. It goes something like this: "Stop looking for happiness in your life and instead look for peace." I took this piece of information and I ran with it. Being happy is great if you can achieve it, but peace I have found is available most of the time. I have much happiness in my life now but only because it is peace that led me there. At first, I found peace hard to find, but I kept working on it. The more I kept my mind focused in the present time and not going back to my past or drifting off to the future and uniting my brain as one, then the more peace came my way. Now I am able to drift off to the past and future and still retain my peace because of the positive network in my brain.

My First Experience with Peace and Hypnosis

The first time I ever discovered peace was under hypnosis, although at the time I was not looking for it and I did not realise it. I had read and heard that hypnosis can be useful. So I looked locally and found a lady who was a registered psychotherapist/hypnotherapist. We spoke for thirty minutes or so, and then it was time to go under. I was only a little bit nervous about hypnosis, but I was sick of anxiety and panic.

Hypnosis was nothing like I expected it to be. I thought I would go under while staring at a silver watch swinging on a chain and then I would wake up at the sound of snapping fingers and remember nothing about it. There was no watch swinging on a chain and no snap of the fingers, just a soothing voice. And I remember much of it, being so relaxed that tears rolled out my eyes. I just listened to this very relaxed, quiet voice and answered all the questions. I clearly remember all the questions relating to how I felt at the time, which I later linked those questions to, discovering peace.

I was so relaxed on a lounge chair, and she asked me, "What do you feel in your body?" I answered, "I feel nothing." She asked, "What do you feel in your legs?" I answered, "I feel nothing." She asked, "What do you feel in your arms?" I answered, "I feel nothing." She asked, "What do you feel in your head?" I answered, "I feel nothing." She asked, "What do you feel in your stomach?" I answered, "I feel nothing." She said to me, "Describe 'nothing.'" I said, "It feels neutral. I don't feel anything." She said, "Describe 'neutral,' and how does it feel?" I said, "It is nothing; it has no pain. I don't feel like I'm happy. I don't feel sad. I just feel nothing." Not long after that, she brought me out of that hypnotic state and we spoke.

Now I can remember that when I arrived I was feeling anxiety, which usually gave me that sick feeling in the stomach. Now I was sitting in a comfortable lounge chair and feeling no anxiety and no pain, feeling "nothing." Just totally relaxed. I came back in two weeks time, and she said, "That will do. See how you go. If you need help in the future, you know where to find me."

My Second Discovery of Peace

At that time, I didn't realise how significant "that feeling of nothing" was. I continued practising all the new skills that I had learnt from reading my books and from hypnotherapy skills, like relaxing, breathing, and clearing the mind, and life was getting better. I continued practising the skill of being in the now, and Eckhart Tolle calls it going inside.

Then one morning I woke up at 2 a.m. Like I always did, I went to the bathroom. But when I came back and lay in bed awake, this time I didn't feel ill like I normally did. I tried going inside so I could fall asleep. It means to relax and clear your mind and take your attention inside your body but I could not fall asleep. Outside hypnotherapy, as I lay in bed that night this was the first time in my life that I had the feeling of "nothing" in my body. That means no pain and no anxiety. I immediately recalled the same sensation under hypnosis. It had been about nine months since my first panic attack, and peace had finally come to me through my own ability.

I related my "feeling of nothing" under hypnosis to my newfound peace that I was experiencing while lying in bed, and they are exactly the same. Peace has no highs and no lows; it has no pain and no joy; it is just like floating in your own body, which is exactly how I felt under hypnosis. I was so pleased to feel no pain that I thanked the universe. Then I thanked myself for persevering.

I believe that being thankful is an important step. It shows that you appreciate your newfound peace and that you did not take it for granted. Plus being thankful always increases your chances next time you ask for something. Being thankful and appreciative is part of my positive snowball, which I believe continues to attract positive things into my life. Peace felt so good that I didn't get back to sleep that night. I was too excited about my new achievement, and in the morning I could not wait to tell my wife of my newfound discovery of peace.

Peace to me is like feeling nothing: zero emotion, zero pain. It is a feeling of space like you are floating in your own space. So how can nothing feel so good? Because all of my life, I now realise, I had anxiety, and from that first panic attack until that night about nine months later, the only relief from anxiety were those brief times under hypnosis. But I discovered my peace came and went. There were times anxiety was in my body and only the occasional glimpse of peace.

Peace in your body is something that has to be continually worked at. You will not find that once you are there you will keep it forever. Anger, your past, or your future will take your peace away in seconds. After I discovered peace at that time, it was all I wanted in life. I stopped looking for happiness. I stopped wanting everything to be perfect. I just wanted my peace. I kept out of anything that disrupted my peace like arguing dramas and opinions. In fact, I became a slightly different person. I preferred to stay in a neutral state. I was not sad, and I was not happy. But my anxiety had mostly left me. I must say that, although I was finding more and more peace, I could have been described as a boring person. But that was OK by me at the time, because I had found peace, and that is so important to me.

After spending a few months in my new peaceful state and with only a hand full of disruptions of anxiety, one night before I drifted off to sleep I gave thanks for my peace. I said to the universe, "I love my peace so much. Can you give me more answers to life?" I said, "Peace has made my life so much better. Could you please open my eyes to more ways to appreciate and love my life?" And with that, I drifted off to sleep. When I woke up in the morning, my body was in peace like it had now become on all the other mornings. I no longer woke up feeling ill. At that point, I smiled and thanked the universe for my peace and for my smile.

Little did I know for the next three days I could not stop smiling. I smiled so much that after one day my face muscles ached; smiling and peace combined are a beautiful combination. So smiling and peace combined have made the past two years since my recovery from panic by far the most beautiful years of my life, with very few disruptions to my peace with no panic attacks and almost no anxiety. Little did I know that peace would lead to joy.

How I Came across Joy in My Life

During the days of panic attacks, it was like a continuous war in my body. And after war in my body, all I wanted was peace so my new destination was peace in my body. That combination of peace then adding the smile opened my eyes even further to discovering joy. Joy in my life was coming. As I felt joy coming my way, it accelerated my positive snowball.

Peace was not given to me easily. I had to change my life to get it. Firstly, I had to commit to the five essential steps to rise above panic attacks. And then in my commitment for a better life I read about important things: don't get involved in drama, stop hating, stop judging, and stop criticizing. Only when I was truly on top of these subjects was I able to learn acceptance, and only when I was able to accept life as it is, did peace come to me. And all this I owe to others.

After a while of living in peace in my new peaceful body, joy did come to me. Joy was not something that I was looking for, but once the smile of joy appeared on my face I felt like I was truly blessed. Joy is just a comfortable feeling of peaceful achievement, and it is so comfortable and so rewarding. Joy is not being happy all the time and it is not exuberance. There is not a buzz with joy, and there is no rush of adrenaline with joy. There is just a very peaceful and quiet sense of having achieved, which comes with only a little smile.

I put together a small equation which explains my joy and why drama, hating, judging, and criticizing are obstacles to it, as well as why acceptance and peace are part of it. It goes like this: "I can't accept something if I hate it or criticise it or judge it, therefore there is no peace and no joy." Once that I have truly overcome these, then I can accept something. And when I learnt acceptance, I gradually found peace and together they became joy. After I lived in peace for a while, joy was a most welcomed by-product, which I did not expect. I thought finding peace was the ultimate, and then a small smile appeared on my face in the shape of joy.

Most people need a reason to smile like hearing a good joke or good news or gaining possession of something. With joy you don't need a reason to smile being alive and loving your life make you smile. And that sense of having achieved peace and you worked it out and made it happen, that's joy.

So I have to spend the next few pages explaining why all these factors are important, but they take a big commitment to change. After you have risen above panic attacks and most of your anxiety, you may want to try to get to joy. I will explain the changes that I needed to make, and they are big changes to what is commonly known as "everyday life."

I learnt that I had to get rid of drama in my life and not accept other people's drama as my own, because I learnt that all drama is negative and it had an effect on me. At the time, I could not understand why watching certain programs or listening to certain media personalities, or even something as simple as following politics, could have an effect on me. But they all did. They triggered my brain when I formed an opinion on them; they left a mark on my subconscious and my brain was no longer one.

Using myself as an example, because I do not want to preach to people what they should or should not do, I will start with violent programs. This was obvious. If I watch violence on television that night, it would turn up in my dreams. An example is that I was watching a comedy late at night and they went to a commercial break that had images of violent scenes and tragedy. That night, I woke up to a nightmare of being involved in that scene, and this was at a time of sleeping through my peaceful nights. This proved to me that watching violence was not for me. There is a lot of drama on television which involves violence, so I choose not to watch it. I also avoid reality programs where people argue fight and criticize.

Dislikes and hates: there are endless amounts of things that I disliked and a few things that I said that I hate. I now realise that disliking something that totally does not involve me or concern me leaves a mark on my subconscious, and actually hating something has an instant effect on me and also leaves a mark on my subconscious. An example of my dislikes are watching television shows, listening to radio programs, and reading newspapers and magazines that continually criticise. One of these mediums would be picking on a person or a section of the community, saying things like "How dare they" and "We are outraged." So there I would be sitting in front of the television, riding on an emotional rollercoaster agreeing with them or arguing against them, and for what? Because I got involved in drama which did not concern or involve me but I used it as entertainment which divided my mind and stopped my peace. What those people were doing or wearing had no effect on my personal life, but now I know because I was on the bandwagon of drama, my subconscious was affected and my brain was no longer one so now I no longer use any of these examples as entertainment.

So now I will cover hating; it's a word that is commonly used to describe things. I said many times, "Oh, I hate this" or "I hate that" or "I can't stand that person." But I'm not alone on this issue. Since I have stopped using these phrases, it is only now that I realise how commonly they are used. So now my subconscious is not scared anymore from my dislikes and petty hates. Hating instantly divides your brain and begins that war in your head that will keep you trapped in your negative network receiving all those negative chemicals from your brain which cause panic anxiety and other illnesses.

Judging and criticising: now this is so simple to explain. Now that my head is clear, I do not like being judged and criticised, so I will not judge or criticise others.

Now onto acceptance. It was only after I genuinely stopped unnecessary drama, and genuinely stopped dislikes and petty hates, and genuinely stopped judging and criticising, that I was able to accept things as they are. I say *genuinely* because if you say it but you don't actually mean it, you will not get to the stage of acceptance and your subconscious and conscious will be at war in your head and not one.

Let me describe what acceptance felt like to me at the time. It felt empty. Yes, empty. I was now able to view television or life or walk down the street or engage in activities without my own comment. Now I was actually able to observe life and see the beauty in it without my own mental noise in my head interfering.

Peace is a beautiful place to be. It felt better than feeling empty. As I described peace earlier in the book, it was a feeling of nothing, no emotion. At first, I only recognised peace when I was sitting or lying still. I would be relaxing on a lounge chair and then I would take my thought inside my body as I was shown to do previously. As my attention went inside my body, at first I would feel that there was no pain in there and I enjoyed it so much. "No pain or anxiety" was all I wanted in life at the time. After a while this feeling inside became so good it felt like I was floating inside my own space, and that feeling was available to me each time I took time out to relax. Eventually, I worked out that this is my meditation. But it got even better than that. Eventually, it didn't matter what I was doing in my life. I could be out and about participating in everyday activity just like everyone else, but if I stopped and paused and took my thought inside, there it was peace. Even if that pause was only a few seconds, my peace was inside. Now the only things that take my peace away from me are drama, dislikes, judging, and criticising because they prevent my brain from being one. As long as I was participating in life without those distractions, I had peace inside. There could be all kinds of problems happening around me, but if it did not involve me or affect me and I did not jump on the drama bandwagon surrounding me, then I had peace inside. When I realised this, it was so rewarding that I just had to smile, and eventually that smile led me to joy.

Joy is now where I spend most of my life, and it is only interrupted by the occasional unavoidable drama.

So staying out of drama leads to my peace, and then that feeling of having achieved peace gives me a small smile which leads to my joy. But it did take a big commitment to change but after you have discovered peace and go on to finding joy the change would have been worth it and there will be no going back to your old ways.

Everything Has Changed, but Nothing Has Changed

There have been so many changes in my life since the panic days that it will need some explaining. But all these changes have taken place inside my body where you cannot see them. The best way for me to explain this is if I use a statement from Eckhart Tolle. He says, "Your life situation is not your life," and from my memory it goes something like this: your "life situation" is what goes on around you like your job and your house your environment and so on, but your "life" is what is inside you. Now I don't want to go over to my bookshelf and quote him word for word, but that is my memory and I do not want to steal his quote. But if you ever get a chance to read it for yourself, you will be better for it. I have discovered that my life is my peace and that is on my inside.

So now we have it. My life is inside me and my life situation is everything around me. I could not have explained it any better. So if my life is so good now inside my peaceful body, then what has changed in my life situation around me to have made it so good? Get ready for this one. The answer is *nothing*. It is only now that I have discovered peace that I am able to open my eyes and see what has always been there. I am still the same person. I still have the same loving wife of thirty years; I still do the same things as I did before the panic and anxiety as I do now. I still look the same. Except for the smile, nothing has changed. But on the inside, my life has changed immensely to peace. The difference is I now look at things positively which has brought peace inside my head, and joy has come into my life which brought peace inside my body. But you cannot see joy around me. It is inside me with my peace and my love for life.

So now all the things that led to panic and anxiety did not change. It is only the way that I look at them that has changed, and that has changed everything. And that is because of my decision to change my thinking and build my new positive network being driven by my positive snowball which united my brain.

Inside this body of mine, there is no longer anxiety 90 percent of the time. Inside my body now, there is peace and joy most of the time. And I realise as much as I would love to have peace and joy 100 percent of the time, I will accept what life gives me, and that is most of the time. As for my friends, they probably will not notice any change. I still look and act very similar; the first time they will hear about my panic and anxiety is if this book ever makes it to a bookshelf. But I love life and everything is beautiful to me; in my internal language, I use the word *beautiful* all the time. If you were to hear my internal language, you might think this guy is nuts, but when I speak out to be heard, I try to say only positive things or nothing at all. But all day long when I'm about to comment on life in a negative way like I did in the old days, my brain will catch me. And my internal language will be, "It's all beautiful." And then I will smile. So in my new life, my mental attitude has changed, but you can't tell that from looking at me. My outlook on life has changed, but you can't see that either. So it is my life that has changed, and that is on the inside.

There have been some health benefits that have come with my peace and joy. All my life I had this nagging cough, which at times would almost choke me. My throat would constrict and I could not swallow. I remember it as a child and as an adult. I coughed and choked to the point of almost passing out. I had been to doctors but was not able to cure it and it was a daily problem in my life. I now call it *stress throat* because in the last two years it has all but gone, and it only appears when times get stressful. And now I can see how common it is among people. I am grateful to have risen above stress throat. I smile most of the time now, and my smile is genuine. I smiled a lot in the anxiety days, but that was to mask what was happening on the inside. I didn't want to look miserable just because I felt that way.

So that is it. Everything changed inside, but nothing has changed on the outside. And when I removed the blindfold of negativity, it revealed that I had all the ingredients of peace; I just had to work out the puzzle for myself which gave me that joyful smile of achievement.

Switching Off and Preventative Maintenance

I think we all have our own personal peace, but not everyone finds it and I am lucky enough to have discovered mine; my peace is inside my body. Through my experience and what I now believe is that my peace lives inside my body, but the path to that peace is through my subconscious mind. If my subconscious mind is not at peace, then my body is not at peace. I have found that I can be using my brain in the now, but I am feeling anxiety and no peace inside because my subconscious is not at peace. That is how I know that my brain and my subconscious mind are two different identities that live in my head. When people say they want peace of mind, I would go one step further and say peace of *subconscious* mind. I found to have a clear mind, I have to have a clear subconscious mind and then my brain is one.

So I have worked hard on clearing the negative images and negative memories of the past. And I work hard on keeping out the negative images and negative thoughts of the present moment. And I work hard on keeping out negative thoughts and negative images of the future. And I work hard on building that positive network into a positive superhighway in my brain. And I do this by building my positive snowball. And I do all this to keep my little mate at peace, and that little mate is my subconscious mind. My little mate is the gate keeper to my peace and he wants to keep that gate open to keep the peace flowing into my body where it so very much appreciated. It is only me when I stray into negativity I disappoint my little mate and the gate to my peace closes then my peace inside is gone so I work hard to keep him happy to keep the gate open and the peace flowing into my body. All this effort is what I call *preventative maintenance* to help keep anxiety away. And I know it is working.

There is a term called *switching off*, which means different things to different people. One description I use is just switching of to negativity using my TRUST image. Another description I use, I have found that I can block out thoughts and stop thinking but only for very short times. Sooner rather than later, my thought process will begin, but the clearer my subconscious is, the shorter the path is through my positive superhighway to where my peace is felt and appreciated, and that is in my body. Remember I said, "Peace is felt in my body, but the path there goes through my mind, my subconscious mind." And my little mate is the gate keeper.

But if I let my mind get caught up in drama, anger, or fear, then the peaceful path to my body is blocked then the gate is closed and my peace is gone and I take responsibility when that happens I never blame my brain or my subconscious. So my personal peace inside depends on me it is not just given to me; I have to work hard on it. Just like working in life, hard work brings rewards, and this reward is peace. Nearly all the hard work that I do is mental work, continuous mental work. I do try to eat and drink healthy foods and do some mild exercise, but mental garbage will override a healthy lifestyle every time. How often have we seen an example of a person who exercises and looks after his health but has a heart attack? That is how powerful mental garbage is. Mental garbage can overwhelm even a healthy lifestyle. It is important to eat and drink well and to do some physical activity, but mental health must also be included.

What I did not know is that negativity to the brain has the same effect as bad food and bad drink to the body. Too much bad food and too much bad drink will affect your physical health everyone knows that. And too much negativity is overwhelming to the brain and it will affect your mental health and very few people know that; but negativity comes disguised as bias, prejudice, hate, ridicule, and contempt and all these close the gate to my peace. There are so many things that are considered normal, but my brain now sees them as negative and I try to avoid them so I can keep my peace and joy. But there is so much of it going around that it is hard work maintaining my peace and joy. But it is hard work that I am prepared to live by. I once thought that negativity is just saying no. I now see it disguised in many other forms that are accepted as normal, everyday living. But that acceptance has no place alongside my acceptance of life, and life is beautiful.

So my preventive maintenance is also keeping away the negativity of everyday living because there is so much of it. I just switch off to it when

I can. I choose to read and watch things that do not take my peace away, and in everyday life where these things are almost unavoidable, I have learnt to switch off to them. Sometimes they may be unavoidable, but I do my best, and if they have left a negative effect on my peace, then that is when I like to have my little quiet times to catch up, sit still, and try to clear my mind. Then I reassure my subconscious and let my peace return through that positive superhighway, which keeps growing in my brain. Also when there are quiet times where I notice my peace or times where life just feels good. I congratulate my little mate on all the progress he has made. Then I thank my beautiful brain and tell it to keep up the good work, and I do this many times per day. It is all part of my preventative maintenance. And I know it works because the more I do it, the less anxiety I get and the more peace and joy I get.

I know that the biggest discovery in my life was discovering my own personal peace and joy, and my maintenance program is about keeping it.

Where I Am at This Stage of My Life

I am referring to peace inside my body. Now that I have sampled peace in my body, I feel like I am on the second rung of a tall ladder that leads to peace and I want to climb to the top of that ladder. Peace in my once anxious body feels so good, and now that I have sampled it, there is no turning back to the old, angry, self-punishing ways that led to panic; they are gone. But there is a lot of work to do and there are still discoveries to be made.

The panic attacks have had a positive effect on my life. When I was struggling with panic and I had dreadful thoughts going through my mind, I said to myself, "I will find a way out, because the alternative is unthinkable."

So I began finding a way out, and around one year later life was back to normal. But I discovered that my normal life needed a lot of work. Not long after that, I came across my positive snowball. The more rewards that came my way—things like peace, love, and joy—and the more that I sampled them, then the more that I wanted them. And I noticed a change is happening inside me. As my anxiety diminishes, I am becoming a better person. This also is building on my positive snowball. I'm finding peace and becoming a better person to be with. My friends have always considered me to be a good guy, but that's why they are friends. I am becoming a better person with my wife and close family, and they are the ones who are usually taken for granted.

Now the biggest friendship I have made is with me. As I became more accepting of myself and my faults, I also become more accepting of life. After I began writing this book, my peace got a wakeup call and some anxiety came my way. But I saw that as a positive thing. Although I love my great new life, there will always be work towards peace. Right now, I know that I am comfortable with what I have written in this book because my peace has returned and I have climbed another rung on that tall ladder that leads to peace.

I have heard people say that we all have a purpose in life, and I agree with that statement. I do believe the panic attacks were a wakeup call to me for a better life, and I am grateful to have experienced them and have now found peace and be where I am both mentally and physically I am definitely better off because I experienced panic attacks. Now I believe my purpose in life is to let other panic-attack sufferers know that there is a way to a better, peaceful life. A lot of what I have written is already out there, but having been through it and by adding my own personal experience, and my knowledge of my brain and my personal discoveries and descriptions and examples, perhaps I have gotten my message across differently. My message is aimed at the panic-attack sufferers who have turned to despair, the ones who have hit rock bottom and have dreadful thoughts going through their heads. If my message is able to help others whose anxiety is not as great as panic attack sufferers then that would be an added joy for me.

I believe that writing this book is what I was meant to do. That is just how I feel. The more that I write, the more comfortable I become with writing. I remember my first trip to my psychotherapist/hypnotherapist I told her about my life and she described me as a rescuer, someone who could not stand by without trying to help. I have seen and heard of people who are struggling mentally where I once was. And in this book I am trying to help, now a quick short story; a weak after we were married we rescued a starving young Dalmatian male dog from the street, he lived a great life with us and brought us much love and joy as our reward for rescuing him. He went back to the universe with a smile on his face at the ripe old age of fifteen his name was Ralph an unforgettable name for me. Helping is helping whether it is humans or animals and it has always been rewarding.

I don't know what the future has in store for me because I like to live in the now. But writing a book demanded that I go back to the past, and I have made a big improvement there. I can now say that I can glimpse the past without anxiety, and even genuinely smile at it, so this book has turned out to be therapy for me. And therapy is aimed at making you more comfortable. I am now more comfortable with myself and with life because of this book.

That is it. My book has now been completed. I hope and TRUST that I have planted a positive seed into your brain for you to build your positive snowball as it continues to build your positive network into a positive superhighway.

So thank you, and keep smiling. Now it's time for me to go back to my quiet, peaceful life.

THE BOOK COVER EXPLAINED

If you have completed reading the book and have wondered about the cover then let me explain my method in its design. I designed it myself with for major ingredients that explain my recovery story from panic attacks to my peaceful smile and once I explain it to you that is if you have not already worked it out for yourself it will become clear. The four ingredients are 1. the thread on the light bulb, 2. the brain, 3. the light and, 4. the smile.

The first ingredient is the thread it is the opposite of a normal light globe. The significance is turn around and do the opposite just because life seems negative when you suffer panic and anxiety it really isn't. So turn the opposite way and become positive just like the world turns from left to right this globe turns the same way.

Step 2. The brain will start to function like it was meant to do and answers will come your way keep your faith in life and trust and believe in it.

Step 3. The next thing is the light will come on in your head and you will wonder why it took you so long to discover the opposite way is the way to the light. Soon life will become so much better you're doing things opposite to your old doubting ways your continually working out how to use your brain the correct positive way and the more you do it the clearer it becomes hence more light comes your way.

Then finally you will be so content with your new found peace that the smile will appear on your face as a permanent fixture and your positive snow ball is well and truly in progress. That's it, all is now explained keep smiling.

Printed in Australia
AUOC010932191012
254151AU00002B/2/P

9 781452 507316

early print copy has mistakes